Three Frames of Modern Politics

Daniel J. McCool

Three Frames of Modern Politics

Self, Others, and Institutions

Daniel J. McCool
Framingham State University
Framingham, MA, USA

ISBN 978-3-319-95647-3   ISBN 978-3-319-95648-0   (eBook)
https://doi.org/10.1007/978-3-319-95648-0

Library of Congress Control Number: 2018954479

Cover credit: CSA-Printstock / Getty Images
Cover design: Fatima Jamadar

This Palgrave Macmillan imprint is published by the registered company Springer Nature Switzerland AG
The registered company address is: Gewerbestrasse 11, 6330 Cham, Switzerland

ACKNOWLEDGMENTS

I express my gratitude to those professors at the CUNY Graduate Center who inspired me to think deeply about the concept of authenticity, both in my academic work and in my own life, especially Joan Richardson and the late great Marshall Berman. Thanks to the Graduate Center students who helped me workshop these ideas between 2011 and 2015: Alan Koenig, Nick Robbins, Joanna Tice, Eli Karetny, and especially Jon Keller. The advice of Tom Halper to "keep punching" at the 26th mile of this project gave me renewed energy to buckle down and finish what I started during a time of adversity. I thank Professors Jeffrey Sedgwick and the late Jerry Mileur of UMass Amherst for helping me through the rigors of my first experience with a major writing project and helping me make the decision to go to grad school. I thank Professor Gerald DeMaio who first hired me at Baruch College when I was twenty-five, beginning employment that supported me throughout my time at NYU and the Graduate Center. I acknowledge Professors Ben Fontana and David Jones for helping me with this book late in the game. I will be forever grateful for the love and patience of partners and friends who were with me along my long academic journey, who often had to accommodate my long, grumpy weekends (and sometimes weeks or months) indoors (and in my own head) with my work, especially the love of my life, Jackie. This would not have been possible without the love, commitment, and encouragement of my family: Mom, Dad, and Jason; I hope this writing and my activities that spring from it carry on the McCool family mission of bringing enlightenment to the world in whatever ways we can. Finally, I'd like to dedicate this book to my mentor at Massasoit Community College, Dr. Tim Trask, who way back in 2002, as Whitman once said of Emerson, brought me to a boil after a long time simmering.

CONTENTS

CHAPTER 1

Introduction: Self, Others, and Institutions

The ideal of authenticity is one of the most common and powerful standards by which modern public actors are judged. At no time and in no place is this stronger today than in American society. As a culture that values authenticity, we attempt to tear off public masks and costumes in order to reveal the intentions and the characters of the individuals underneath. Public actors, in both government and everyday society, are expected to act outwardly in line with what they "really" feel, think, or intend or else they are deemed illegitimate. Politicians must convey transparency, intimacy, and unity in their characters. These internal traits are seen as more important than the external institutions within which politicians must work in order to actually get anything done. There are many examples of this. George W Bush's acceptance speech at the 2004 Republican National Convention echoed a theme that was repeated by campaign operatives in order to contrast him with the "flip-flopping" John Kerry to great effect. "In the last four years," Bush confided, as if talking to a friend, "you and I have come to know each other. Even when we don't agree, at least you know what I believe and where I stand."[1] The strategy behind the 2012 presidential campaign of Barack Obama relied on this same standard, as White House senior advisor David Plouffe accused Mitt Romney on Meet the Press of having "no core."[2] This constant charge of inauthenticity by the Obama campaign prompted several feckless defenses of Romney's character, including one by a member of his gubernatorial administration in Massachusetts: "I could tell immediately,

© The Author(s) 2019
D. J. McCool, *Three Frames of Modern Politics*,
https://doi.org/10.1007/978-3-319-95648-0_1

just by our interaction, that he is the real thing—authentic! He struck me then—and now—as honest, transparent and inclusive."[3] While this attempt by the Romney campaign and its surrogates proved futile, the effort alone shows how important it is for politicians to seem authentic. And during the 2016 election, the candidate who received the highest score on "authenticity" in public opinion polls was none other than Donald J Trump.[4]

The ideal of authenticity is not one relegated to electoral politics. In non-political matters of public life, especially in celebrity culture, we have been trained to peer behind the words of public actors, into their minds, their souls, their very selves to determine their level of sincerity. When public figures are judged by their authenticity and sincerity, their legitimacy is measured not primarily by what they say or do, but by whether or not they believe in what they say or do. The modern mass public displaces judgment away from outward acts and onto the individual's character, intention, sincerity, and, importantly, whether such feelings are prideful and self-serving (and thus illegitimate) or humble self-sacrificing (and thus legitimate). Focus on the internal life is not an exclusively modern phenomenon. Indeed, some of the most celebrated figures in Western history have been praised on such grounds. Socrates, the seminal figure in the history of Western political thought, stands in front of the jury in the *Apology*, without attempting to manipulate their judgment with the presence of his weeping family, and professes that the sincerity of his words are a testament to his commitment to virtues of justice and truth larger than himself.[5] We see this kind of authentic self-sacrifice play out in the story of Christ and other martyrs from Western history. What is new in modern society is the source from which the virtue of authenticity is seen to emerge and the polity it is supposed to help create. In the ancient and medieval worlds, the authentic self was compelled to be privately authentic and publicly sincere by cosmic forces that governed a well-ordered universe.[6] Often, this meant creating monarchical or aristocratic societies that had vertically organized power structures. In modernity, the authentic self is supposed to be compelled from within to tell the truth and remain steadfast in one's beliefs no matter the consequences. Often, this is in service of creating democratic societies, in which people live together in egalitarian ways.

Aloneness, Authenticity, Democracy

The moral standard of authenticity that we apply to public figures, in which the inner self matches the presentation of the outer self, is a relatively new one in world history. It has become a staple of modern life, and is engrained in our politics, art, music, and advertising. In his book *Sincerity*, Jay Magill gives a thumbnail view of how the virtues of authenticity and sincerity have woven their ways throughout our modern culture:

> Over the decades, this ethos of sincerity evolved from seeking the truth of oneself to sharing the whole of that truth with others with unabashed pride, a trait that would come to be called, in modern times, authenticity. This insistence on being who one feels oneself to be at all times eventually found a home in modern art and literature. Artists and writers well into the twentieth century, following Rousseau, declared the importance of the self's authenticity against the inauthenticity of modern consumer society, which many critics believed had enslaved individuals in a capitalist system and then offered them an illusory freedom through the purchase of its products. The line of criticism and rebellious self-expressiveness has rolled into our own time, of course, through art, music, fashion, and literature—through Beats and hippies and punk and rap—and eventually through the messages of some of the world's largest advertising agencies and corporations ....[7]

Why did this ideal of authenticity become so ubiquitous in the modern world? Many have answered that it stems from the phenomenon of aloneness. With the breakdown of the family, the onslaught of capitalism, the promise of the emancipation of the self from social bonds, and the radical centering of religious life on the self, individuals found themselves cutoff from ties to external persons and institutions that had given earlier peoples their identities. This type of aloneness created an absence of public politics. As Charles Taylor describes it, the combination of these forces created "a society of self-fulfillers, whose affiliations are more and more seen as revocable" which "cannot sustain the strong identification with the political community which public freedom needs."[8] Modern thinkers had to come up with new theories of politics and community that took as a given the atomization of the self.

In the modern world, aloneness has been the problem with which we each grapple while authenticity has been the state of being to which we each aspire. While in some ways we wish to be left alone to develop our unique lives and personalities from within, we also seek community in which that uniqueness can be displayed. This combination of an authentic self with an intimate community is a quintessentially modern one that found its highest expression in the twentieth century. At the height of "the 1960s" in America, political theorist Marshall Berman wrote about "both the dignity and agony of aloneness" in connecting the personal trait of authenticity with the political system of democracy:

> The way to democracy that the Enlightenment developed, and that millions of people in the 1960s experienced anew, was a distinctively modern way. It meant people coming together from a matrix of solitude, people breaking out of an existential loneliness. This loneliness was completely missing from the culture of ancient democracy. But it is a central modern experience … Two millennia of Christian domination have not only legitimized aloneness, they have sanctified it and given it an aura; this aura touches everyone, Christian or not. One of the Enlightenment's main tasks was to establish a secular foundation for a right to privacy. The eighteenth century, like the twentieth, produced generations deeply and often happily immersed in private life that demanded new, democratic forms of public life. From Rousseau, above all, we can learn both the dignity and agony of aloneness, and the yearning for a new form of community. What kind of community should it be? A community that instead of absorbing and crushing the self will recognize and affirm it; a community where everybody will be open about their identity and welcome—eagerly, even—the opportunity to confess who and what they are; where every individual can 'expand his being and multiply his happiness by sharing them with his fellow men.' Some thinkers argue that these values are contradictory and incompatible. 'The politics of authenticity' makes the impossible demand to realize them all at once.[9]

Berman, by employing his prized example of Jean-Jacques Rousseau, makes links between achieving one's authentic self and a democracy in which that self is able to be expressive.

Elsewhere, in *All That Is Solid Melts into Air*, Berman employs the early modern tragedy of Shakespeare's King Lear to create a seamless web between authenticity, humanity, empathy, and ultimately democratic community. After King Lear is stripped of political power (and significantly, the royal vestments that go along with it) and thrown out into the street to face "the naked truth [of] what man is forced to face when he has lost everything," he recognizes a connection between himself and another human being. This recognition enables him to grow in sensitivity and insight, and to move beyond the bounds of his self-absorbed bitterness and misery. As he stands and shivers, it dawns on him that his kingdom is full of people whose whole lives are consumed by the abandoned, defenseless suffering that he is going through right now ... Shakespeare is telling us that the dreadful naked reality of the 'unaccommodated man' is the point from which accommodation must be made, the only ground on which real community can grow.[10]

While Americans do not consciously search for revolutionary correctives to our existential problems of aloneness, what Berman describes in Lear is what we expect today from our politicians in return for granting them political legitimacy: that they disrobe from their veils, vestiges and masks of office, title, and social distinction to—as was famously repeated in Bill Clinton's 1992 presidential campaign—"feel our pain." The politics of authenticity holds that only with this transparency between politicians and the people, and then among the people themselves, do we have a true democracy.

Other modern thinkers have railed against the politics of authenticity, believing that politics ought not be a reflection of the inner life at all. While we often equate democracy with the protection and promotion of individual realization within the self, it has not always been thus. In an essay in which she lauds the freedom of ancient Greek citizens, political theorist Hannah Arendt harkens back to an ancient conception of freedom not as a private or personal matter, but fundamentally as a public one, constituted outside the individual self in "the world":

[i]n spite of the great influence the concept of an inner, non-political freedom has exerted upon the tradition of thought, it seems safe to say that man would know nothing of inner freedom if he had not first experienced a condition of being free as a worldly tangible reality. We first become aware of freedom or its opposite in our intercourse with others, not in the intercourse with ourselves. Before it became an attribute of thought or a quality of the will, freedom was understood to be the free man's status, which enabled him to move, to get away from home, to go out into the world and meet other people in deed and word. Freedom needed ... the company of other men who were in the same state, and it needed a common public space to meet them—a politically organized world, in other words, into which each of the free men could assert himself by word and deed.[11]

The Loss of Self

Normative political models differ on the relative importance of private and public life. But most modern political thinkers have been concerned with the same anxieties: the disintegration, the colonization, or the simple loss of "the self," as they conceive it. They have feared that instead of defining themselves, men and women would blindly follow the opinions of others and other social forces that demanded group cohesion and destroyed individuality. During the rise of the "common man" in Jacksonian America, for example, Tocqueville warned that the rising power of democratic public opinion would crush individuality. The fear of being alone would compel individuals to become conformists:

> Tyranny in democratic republics does not proceed [as it used to]... It ignores the body and goes straight for the soul. The master no longer says: You will think as I do or die. He says: You are free not to think as I do. You may keep your life, your property, and everything else. But from this day forth you shall be as a stinger among us. You will retain your civic privileges, but they will be of no use to you. For if you seek the votes of your fellow citizens, they will withhold them, and if you seek only their esteem, they will feign to refuse even that. You will remain among men, but you will forfeit your rights to humanity. When you approach your fellow creatures, they will shun you as one who is impure. And even those who believe in your innocence will abandon you, lest they, too, be shunned in turn. Go in peace, I will not take your life, but the life I leave you with is worse than death.[12]

A half century later, Nietzsche was already writing the postmortem on the possibilities for modern individuality. A modern culture that valued it so much paradoxically tended to do away with it:

> The modern spirit, with its restlessness, its hatred for bounds and moderation, has come to dominate every domain, at first let loose by the fever of revolution and then, when assailed by fear and horror of itself, again laying constraints upon itself.[13]

The emergence of "mass society" in the nineteenth and twentieth centuries spawned a new series of critiques of this conformist modern self, especially from the Frankfurt School. Horkheimer and Adorno lamented the rise of the "culture industry" which homogenized culture, manipulated the mass public, and robbed people of their individuality.[14] In *Escape from Freedom,* Erich Fromm echoes Nietzsche's characterization of modern individuals' self-imposed captivity, when individuals accept conformity and authoritarianism in the face of political and existential groundlessness. Like many midcentury critics who worried about escapes from freedom, Fromm thought modern individuals were not really free, but that they were "happy slaves" as Rousseau referred to bourgeois individuals in the eighteenth century. Fromm applies this fear to the highly valued American right of free speech:

> Although freedom of speech constitutes an important victory in the battle against old restraints, modern man is in a position where much of what 'he' thinks and says are the things that everybody else thinks and says; that he has not acquired the ability to think originally—that is, for himself—which alone gives meaning to his claim that nobody can interfere with the expression of his thoughts.[15]

Not only do we unconsciously follow the herd, but we actively fear and escape freedom:

> The frightened individual seeks for somebody or something to tie his self to, he cannot bear to be his own individual self any longer, and he tries frantically to get rid of it and to feel security again by the elimination of this burden: the self.[16]

Like many thinkers who express anxiety over modern self-abandonment, Fromm's corrective is self-realization:

> We forget that, although each of the liberties which have been won must be defended with utmost vigor, the problem of freedom is not only a quantitative one, but a qualitative one; that we not only have to preserve and increase the traditional freedom, but that we have to gain a new kind of freedom, one which enables us to realize our own individual self; to have faith in this self and in life.[17]

Postwar critiques of the modern self from critics like David Riesman and Nathan Glazer painted an even bleaker picture for the possibility for individual autonomy. They focus on the rise of the suburbs, the bureaucratic state, and an advanced industrialized world that characterized an even more homogenized mass society in which individuals became increasingly "other-directed."[18] Individuals came to completely rely on the fashions, opinions, and consumer behaviors of others for their own shallow identities. While a bounty of consumer products satiated biological needs to create a comfortable life, the self was psychologically lost in conformity. Worse, driving this conformity was the hidden, mostly unconscious pressure from peers:

> [s]table and individualistic pursuits are today being replaced by the fluctuating tastes which the other-directed person accepts from his peer-group. Moreover, many of the desires that drove men to work and to madness in societies depending on inner-direction are now satisfied relatively easily; they are incorporated into the standard of living taken for granted by millions. But the craving remains.[19]

The shallowness, conformity, and external role-playing of this postwar lifestyle became the backdrop for the critique of the New Left. The Port Huron Statement issued by Students for a Democratic Society argued that "[t]he goal of man and society should be human independence: a concern not with image of popularity but with finding a meaning in life that is personally authentic."[20] Betty Friedan presented a picture of existential meaninglessness American women faced in their own externally defined roles:

> Each suburban wife struggles with [meaninglessness] alone. As she made the bed, shopped for groceries, matched slipcover material, ate peanut butter sandwiches with her children, chauffeured Cub Scouts and Brownies, lay beside her husband at night—she was afraid to ask even of herself, 'Is this all?'[21]

Since the rise of the New Left in the 1960s, personal authenticity was lauded as the outward expression of an inner voice that had been hidden by external pressures and oppressions. Each vision of authenticity then led to some vision of an intimate democratic, egalitarian society populated by citizens who privately realize and then publicly express themselves. This connection between authentic personal discovery and a democratic public space for that expression can be summarized in the famous feminist assertion that "the personal is political."

The absence of a sovereign self often coincided with the absence of a political voice that could affect change through complex political institutions. Thus, recovery of the self often took place outside of formal institutions, and indeed, in direct opposition to them. Today's political language, in which politicians rail "against the establishment" and even promise to "drain the swamp" on behalf of the common people, took root in this 1960s New Left discourse. Today, however, while this discourse of authenticity is used on all sides of the political spectrum, it is more prevalent on the populist right, which has co-opted the language of anti-establishment self-assertion, and self-recovery, from the left, especially in the age of Trumpism.

THE BOOK

This book will detail three different views of modern politics, and how they have developed over time. It starts by detailing two opposing models of modern politics that stem from anxiety over the loss of self: the politics of authenticity, and the politics of theatricality. While both authentic and theatrical politics express anxiety about the loss of self in the modern world, they disagree firstly on what the self is; secondly, on how it was lost; and thirdly, on how to reconstitute it. Thus, we will explore how these different models address each. While describing these models, we will then then look at how, in their individualistic extremes, each leads to a dangerous ignorance of political institutions that seek to mitigate common public disputes, leading to an anarchic anti-politics, in which the fashioning of the self is the only thing that matters in public life. We'll consider how Henry David Thoreau finds a way to mix the best of both models in his unique and robust style of politics. As a corrective to the anarchic states that these models can engender in the extreme, we'll explore the foundations of a third model—institutional politics—against which both the New Left and the populist right have defined themselves since the 1960s. Finally, we'll consider the ways in which the discourse of authenticity in particular has become of a staple of the populist right.

THE THEORISTS

The main representatives for the opposing political models of authenticity and theatricality will be Jean-Jacques Rousseau and Hannah Arendt. For institutional politics, we will explore the writings of modern thinkers like Montesquieu, Locke, Martin Diamond, Madison, and Lincoln. And for conservatism, we will explore Edmund Burke's writings. Henry David Thoreau will be presented as the thinker with whom we can find a healthy synthesis of authentic and theatrical politics. We will bring all of these theoretical considerations to bear on contemporary politics, particularly the sort practiced by today's populist right. Methodologically, I take direction from the "transhistorical" method described by Michael Frazier.[22] This method seeks to use the canon of great books for practical wisdom, rather than understanding works exclusively as products of their time and place. In other words, I take for granted that what Rousseau has to say about the relationship between human nature and political institutions, for instance, is still as applicable today as it was in the time and place he wrote it.

In Rousseau's politics of authenticity, the emergence of the bourgeois public sphere does not usher in a new age of individual freedom. Instead, bourgeois individuals define themselves based on what they perceive others think of them. In order to gain the favor of others, they perform public personas that mimic others. As the donning of this other-directed mask becomes a way of life, their private selves are submerged below the surfaces of the personae they become. Yet, behind the public persona rests the latent, internal potential for autonomy and conscientious compassion. They are split in two. This "doubleness" of the bourgeois that Rousseau laments is evidenced in the splitting of the false, public persona from the authentic hidden, private realm where autonomy and compassion persist, however remotely.

Rousseau's corrective to this self-alienation is to unify the outer persona with the inner self. He achieves this, in *Emile* and in his autobiographical works, by first cultivating these traits within the individual before he enters the public realm. Having regained one's potential for natural autonomy and compassion, one is then equipped to live with others without giving up one's selfhood. Individuals will no longer perform the mimicry of a public persona they adopt from others but will express their individual consciences instead. We see that Rousseau's politics of authenticity unifies the self by bringing together the latent goodness of the individual with its subsequent outward manifestation in the public sphere. The personal and public dimensions of the self are thus collapsed into one unified, authentic subject.

Arendt's politics of theatricality argues that Rousseau has aided in depoliticizing the modern world by shifting the focus of politics from the public to the private realm. Under the politics of authenticity, public judgment and governmental coercion are focused on the hidden, private intentions of individual actors rather than on the visible acts they perform in public. The erosion of the public sphere has left mass man no space in which to individuate oneself among others. The lack of the public sphere leads to the destruction of the private sphere. Men and women have been cut off from the "common sense" one needs to experience with others to confirm one's very existence as an individual. Arendt refers to this experience of the loss of self as "loneliness." Totalitarian ideologies then exploit loneliness by giving the individual solutions to existential malaise that promise new grounding. Men and women are reduced to automatons without the ability to think or act.

As a corrective, Arendt offers a politics that reestablishes the division between the private and public dimensions of the self in order to protect the integrity of each. In the private realm, Arendt promotes thinking in solitude as the "two-in-one." This is a private inner dialogue in which one "internalizes the audience" of the outside world before acting in the public realm among others. This differs from the Rousseauist variant of prepolitical solitude, which requires one to be cut off from the influence of public opinion in order to achieve autonomy. In the public realm, Arendt celebrates a theatrical politics. The mask or persona of each public actor gives one a common status among equals. The public actor can then individuate oneself by performing heroic words and deeds that are recognized by one's audience. The mask also serves the function of protecting the private self from external public judgment or governmental coercion.

Like Rousseau and Arendt, Thoreau seeks a politics that equips the self with the ability to achieve individuality, both when alone and when acting in public. Throughout his writings he recognizes and then resists what Jane Bennett calls "the They" within himself. In order to achieve this, Thoreau alternates between Rousseauist and Arendtian modes of politics. At times he rejects the mimicry of others by leaving the public realm to rediscover his individual nature in private. At other times he individuates himself among others by performing a persona to public audiences. In both his private writings and his public actions, he transcends the tension between Rousseau's collapsing of the private and public dimensions of the self and Arendt's strict division between those dimensions.

Thoreau exhibits strong Rousseauist features when he writes about the recovery of his authentic individuality. Like Rousseau's autobiographical works, Walden gives readers an exposé into Thoreau's self-recovery by cataloguing his daily thoughts and activities in solitude. There are passages from Walden in which Thoreau recognizes that the development of his own unique individuality would not be possible if he were subjected to bombardment from public opinion in town among his neighbors. Thoreau also exhibits Rousseauist features in "Civil Disobedience." Here, he writes about how his inner conscience is the motivation for his public actions. By expressing his conscience to the community, he blurs the line dividing his private world of conscience and his public persona in an attempt to provoke others to listen to their own consciences.

In other ways, Thoreauvian politics contains prominent Arendtian features. While Walden allows a window into the Thoreau's private thoughts and activities, he resists going the full Rousseauist route of expressive intimacy by creating buffers between himself and his readers. Spatially, Walden Pond is "one mile from any neighbor" which, as Cavell notes, is "just far enough to be seen clearly."[23] Much like the function achieved by Arendt's conception of a public mask, Thoreau's one-mile distance serves as a buffer between him and his audience, yet it is also close enough for his voice to "sound through" to his readers. In a passage from Walden, he details the necessity of "sufficient distance" between individuals so that they "have considerable neutral ground between them" for their "sentences to unfold." Behind Thoreau's obscured literary persona, he is engaged in the process of thinking, which, as he notes in Walden, contains a "certain doubleness." We can see that this is not unlike the "two-in-one" Arendt celebrates in her Socratic theory of thinking.

Both Rousseauist and Arendtian features are contained in Thoreau's more explicitly political writings. In his most famous political writing "Civil Disobedience," Thoreau calls his audience's attention to his private conscience in order to provoke theirs. But in a lesser known speech called "A Plea for Captain John Brown," he uses an Arendtian mode of political performance not in order to express his inner conscience but to create a public object for judgment by using shocking rhetorical imagery about John Brown's Christ-like qualities. While it may have been motivated by Thoreau's inner conscience, Thoreau directs his audience's judgment not to his own moral law within but to an object outside and between himself and his readers: the great and heroic deeds of John Brown.

Like Thoreau, in the writings and speeches of Abraham Lincoln, we see an oscillation between an authentic self, expressing an inner conscience, and a performing stage actor playing a role, pleasing and provoking an audience. With Lincoln however, we see the added benefit of providing institutional grounding for these modes of politics in his reverence for "civil religion," which Thoreau had not fully developed in his politics. Lincoln provides a way for us to think about institutional politics in his own day of civil discord, which takes account of the need for theatrics and persuasion, as well as stable moral fortitude. This politics seeks ways to avoid the extremes of either model by providing stable, predictable laws, institutions, and procedures by which disparate groups can resolve disputes. In the early modern period, this meant replacing the governmental authority of inheritance and titles with that of functionality and impersonal laws. We will explore the ways in which *The Federalist Papers* lay the foundation for institutional politics in the United States.

Finally, we will look at the populist right's co-opting of anti-institutionalist politics. We will trace an intellectual history from Edmund Burke to twentieth-century conservative institutionalists to see how the right has served as a counterrevolutionary force. But we will explore how the New Left's discourse of authenticity in the 1960s became a staple of Reaganism and then, even more so, Trumpism. From there, we will conclude by discussing some modern ideological movements, in addition to Trumpism, that have been fueled by anti-institutionalism, and the ways in which we can rethink the interplay of authenticity, theatricality, and institutionalism going forward.

OTHER MODERN DISCOURSES

The tension between authentic politics and the theatrical politics runs parallel to other classic debates in political theory. Many times (but not all the time), the assumptions of each side of these other debates are the same assumptions held by authentic and theatrical politics. The old tension between republicanism and liberalism is one example of the ways in which the authenticity vs. theatricality debate can expand beyond the narrow foci of each. While both liberalism and republicanism share a belief in individual freedom, they weigh it differently against the need for community and collective action. In their ideal types, liberalism tends to prioritize individual liberty, privacy, commerce, competition, and shuns too much intimacy and collective action. Republicanism prioritizes community, transparency, virtue, and cooperation and encourages the development of bonds of civic friendship in collective action while favoring simpler, more directly democratic forms of government. This tension was especially pointed, for example, during the debates between the Federalists and Anti-Federalists over the US Constitution. The liberal Federalists assumed much from theatrical politics, and favored a complex form of government that would encourage commercialism, competition, and physical and fraternal distance between citizens. The republican Anti-Federalists took their cues from a more authentic politics, and thought the dynamism of the Federalists would destroy virtue and the bonds of citizenship, leading the way to a shallow society of alienated selves. This could, they argued, unleash various forms of tyranny that exploited a depoliticized population. In Cato's fifth letter, he warns that "the progress of a commercial society begets luxury, the parent of inequality, the foe to virtue"[24] For the republican Anti-Federalists—like we shall see for theorists of authenticity from romantic, Enlightenment auto-critics to the counter-culture hippies of the 1960s—too much artificiality in a hyper-commercialized society kills the natural virtue within the self, leading to social inequality, lack of compassion among citizens, and a host of other undemocratic ills. For the liberal Federalists, coalitions of citizens that were too democratic, and thus too tightly knit, would lead to a tyranny of the majority and, by extension, the loss of individual freedom.

Political theorists have sought ways to join the benefits of both liberalism and democracy, each of which makes different assumptions about how opaque or how intimate citizens should be toward one another. Thomas Dumm writes in his book *Loneliness as a Way of Life* that ideally democracy and liberalism can "enable each other," constituting "a marvelously rich matrix, a culture for living our life in common and in solitude."[25] This is a tension that we will explore in depth when discussing authentic vs. theatrical politics and how each of them relates to the totalitarian loneliness that the masses faced in the twentieth century. Dumm attempts to approach this "matrix" in which togetherness and aloneness, the self and the community, and, ultimately, liberalism democracy might thrive in tandem in our age. The way in which we will approach this problem in this book is through the debate between authenticity, which argues for transparency and intimacy among individual selves in a community, and theatricality, which argues for opacity and distance between citizens who are joined only through impersonal political institutions and processes.

Still, the fact that the separateness vs. togetherness of modern citizens can be framed in different ways begs the question: why is a debate between the politics of authenticity vs. the politics of theatricality important? The reasons are several. Firstly, it is a rich debate that spans the last several centuries since the Enlightenment. No one has written an intellectual history on this precise tension. And while this book is not a precise chronological history of the debate between authenticity and theatrical politics, it seeks to provide a theoretical framework with which one could begin if one wished to write such a history.

Secondly, extreme versions of authenticity and theatricality are rampant in American political society today, and that is a problem for a stable liberal democracy. Americans have an alarming lack of faith in public, deliberative institutions, both governmental and non-governmental, and that continues to worsen. In its stead, we've seen the rise of "tell-it-like-it-is" authentic politics, which moves politics out of the public realm and into the private, combined with a theatrical politics that focuses on shock value without substance. Thus, our political debates have been reduced to competing symbolic performances—exacerbated by our culture wars—rather than a genuine debate about political problems and solutions. This toxic blend of the worst aspects of authenticity and theatricality has created the potential for lawless authoritarianism, in which the personalities, motives, and shallow political stunts of political actors command our public attention, drawing us further away from the institutions that were created to peacefully resolve our grievances. Public erosion in support for institutions does not just apply to Congress, the presidency, and the courts, but also to journalism, academia, science, and specialized experts that are supposed to provide facts and evidence that a liberal democratic society relies upon to debate honestly. The self-fashioning and self-expression that must take place among large groups of citizens in any free society, movements for justice and inclusion that stem from those self-projects, and the somewhat disempowering role that complex institutions play in the lives of those citizens require a delicate balance that we are failing to achieve. Yascha Mounk presents the problem this way:

> In order to govern effectively, nearly every democracy has thus established more and more technocratic institutions. Experts figure out how to regulate power plants. Bureaucratic agencies pass many more binding rules than parliaments. International organizations try to coordinate the actions of different states in areas in which the whole world needs to work together. But taken together, the effect of all of these developments has been to make many citizens feel as though their vote doesn't really matter. And they have a point: It's really difficult to see, for example, how individual voters can have any meaningful effect on something as vast and complicated as the international response we need to climate change.

> Now, some elites want to say that none of this is a problem: So long as these institutions do good work, we shouldn't worry about them. On the other hand, many populists suggest a simplistic solution: Abolish these institutions, return power to the people, everything will be hunky-dory. The reason I call this a genuine dilemma is that I don't think either of these views is

convincing. We do genuinely need some of these technocratic institutions. But at the same time, they do genuinely disempower the people. This is a fundamental challenge for our political system—and I don't see an easy way out of it.[26]

By exploring the ways in which modern thinkers have thought about self-alienation, perhaps we can shed light on the malaise that American citizens feel today, and start to think about ways to find the balance between political self-expression in the name of justice, whether authentic or theatrical, and the need for institutional mechanisms to temper our darker political instincts.

In the end, this book seeks to generate thinking into what the possibilities are for politics in twenty-first-century America and how might we, as selves, achieve them. This book does not answer all these questions completely, but it attempts to give us a framework to do so. By investigating other theories and moments in history that seek to find a home for the self in a complex, often alienating public world, we can elucidate our own political and existential predicaments and, hopefully, reimagine new ways that both the inner self and community-oriented citizenship might flourish in our liberal democracy.

NOTES

1. George W. Bush, "President Bush's Acceptance Speech to the Republican National Convention," *The Washington Post*, September 2, 2004, http://www.washingtonpost.com/wp-dyn/articles/A57466-2004Sep2.html.
2. Tom Cohen, "Romney Remains the Top Target of GOP Rivals, White House," *CNN*, October 30, 2011, https://www.cnn.com/2011/10/30/politics/romney-targeted/index.html.
3. Jane Edmonds, "Jane Edmonds at the 2012 Republican National Convention," *C-SPAN Video Library*, August 23, 2012, https://www.c-span.org/video/?307604-1/republican-national-convention-day-four.
4. Greg Sargent, "Who is the 'Authenticity' Candidate of 2016? Yup: It's Donald Trump," *The Washington Post*, December 11, 2015, https://www.washingtonpost.com/blogs/plum-line/wp/2015/12/11/who-is-the-authenticity-candidate-of-2016-yup-its-donald-trump/.
5. see Plato, *Apology of Socrates* (Warminster: Aris & Phillips, 1997).
6. Charles Taylor, *Sources of the Self: The Making of the Modern Identity* (Cambridge, MA: Harvard UP, 1989), 321.

7. Magill, R. Jay, *Sincerity: How a Moral Ideal Born Five Hundred Years Ago Inspired Religious Wars, Modern Art, Hipster Chic, and the Curious Notion That We All Have Something to Say (no Matter How Dull)* (New York: Norton, 2012), 21.
8. Taylor, *Sources of the Self,* 508.
9. Marshall Berman, *The Politics of Authenticity: Radical Individualism and the Emergence of Modern Society* (London: Verso, 2009), xiii.
10. Marshall Berman, *All That Is Solid Melts into Air: The Experience of Modernity* (New York: Simon and Schuster, 1982), 107–08.
11. Hannah Arendt, "What Is Freedom?" in *The Portable Hannah Arendt* (New York: Penguin Books, 2000), 442.
12. Alexis De Tocqueville, *Democracy in America*, trans. Arthur Goldhammer (New York: Library of America, 2004), 294.
13. Friedrich Wilhelm Nietzsche. *Human, All Too Human*, trans. R. J. Hollingdale (Cambridge: Cambridge UP, 1996), 103.
14. Max Horkheimer and Theodore Adorno, *Dialectic of Enlightenment: Philosophical Fragments*, ed. Gunzelin Schmid Noerr, trans. Edmund Jephcott (Stanford, CA: Stanford UP, 2002), 97.
15. Erich Fromm, *Escape from Freedom* (New York: H. Holt, 1994), 105.
16. Fromm, *Escape*, 151.
17. Fromm, *Escape*, 110.
18. David Riesman, Nathan Glazer and Reuel Denney, *The Lonely Crowd: A Study of the Changing American Character* (New Haven, CT: Yale University Press, 2001).
19. Riesman, Glazer and Denney, *Lonely Crowd*, 79.
20. Students for a Democratic Society "The Port Huron Statement" in *American Political Thought*, ed. Kenneth M. Dolbeare (Chatham, NJ: Chatham House, 1998), 490.
21. Betty Friedan, *The Feminine Mystique* (New York: W.W. Norton, 1963), 1.
22. Michael Frazier, "The Methods of Political Theory: Historicism, Ahistoricism, and Transhistoricism." Paper presented at the *Canadian Political Science Association Annual Meeting, June 1, 2010*. https://www.cpsa-acsp.ca/papers-2010/Frazer.pdf.
23. Stanley Cavell, *The Senses of Walden* (Chicago: University of Chicago, 1992), 11.
24. George Clinton, "Cato Letter V," in *The Antifederalists*, by Cecelia M. Kenyon (Indianapolis: Bobbs-Merrill, 1976), 308–09.
25. Thomas Dumm, *Loneliness as a Way of Life* (Cambridge, MA: Harvard UP, 2008), 31.
26. David Frum, "If America's Democracy Fails, Can Other Ones Survive?," *The Atlantic*, March 4, 2018, https://www.theatlantic.com/international/archive/2018/03/yascha-mounk-democracy/554786/.

CHAPTER 2

The Politics of Authenticity

In this chapter we'll explore the connection between personal authenticity and how it interacts with movements for justice and inclusion in the modern world. In so doing, we will take a somewhat sympathetic view toward the politics of authenticity, as a discourse through which oppressed people can interrupt theatrical and institutional norms, and assert their humanity into the political realm. As with Socrates and other pre-modern social and political reformers, this discourse attempts to dig below conventions and appearances, to get the self to know itself, and to achieve transparency between the self and others, and between society and governing institutions. Beneath the false consciousness of the self, there are both dark motives and unrealized potential for happiness and for political agency that could be unleashed. Behind the role-playing of other people are these same latent traits. And behind seemingly fair and open economic and political systems are spaces for dominance and exploitation that must be brought to the attention of the public. The politics of authenticity is thus not merely about self-realization, but engages in *uncovering* of social and political masks and costumes that often hide systemic abuses. Advocates for authenticity are willing to create public spaces that were previously considered private if they believe they harbor or instigate injustice, or if publicizing private spaces makes a contribution to what they consider a more just democratic sphere. Thus, we'll see an intimate connection between radical self-actualization and communitarian democracy.

© The Author(s) 2019
D. J. McCool, *Three Frames of Modern Politics,*
https://doi.org/10.1007/978-3-319-95648-0_2

We can understand the politics of authenticity by laying out its metaphysical worldview from its foundational writers and from real-world events. The most celebrated proponent of this metaphysics was Jean-Jacques Rousseau. As American constitutional law professor Nelson Lund tells us, Rousseau is an important figure in the history of Western thought:

> No modern philosopher has been more influential than Rousseau, or more misunderstood. There is scarcely a modern intellectual or political movement whose seeds cannot be seen, rightly or wrongly, in some aspect of Rousseau's thought—the French Revolution, communism, fascism, contemporary communitarianism, as well as the politics of compassion and political leaders who take on the role of public comforters.[1]

Others who contributed to the politics of authenticity include Martin Luther, Karl Marx, and, in America, as I argue, Frederick Douglass, Elizabeth Cady Stanton, and some of the New England Transcendentalists. We can also see the importance of the politics of authenticity in the American and French Revolutions, in Jacksonian politics, and in the social movements of the 1960s. To break the formalism of the *ancien régime* and of bourgeois society, the Jacobins had to strip away its costumes to reveal the self. To uncover the dehumanization of American slavery, Douglass had to show himself as a real human being. Stanton, similarly, had to base her arguments on her biographical experiences of oppression to uncover and challenge patriarchy. And the Transcendentalists had to reconnect deeply with a sense of self in order to protest the shallowness of a bustling commercial society in America. Authenticity has also been employed on the right by reactionaries and conservatives like Father Coughlin, Pitchfork Ben Tillman, Ronald Reagan, Sarah Palin, and, most recently, Donald Trump. Like for their predecessors on the left, authenticity signaled an emancipation from formalisms and costumes of polite society. Across the spectrum, to be perceived as authentic, especially in American political culture, is to be perceived as a legitimate public actor. The populist's favorite tool in combatting the status quo has always been to "get real" with his or her audience while at the same time, the audience seems to understand itself as "real" through the address of the speaker.

Rousseau is the modern father of the discourse. A philosopher, writer, and, at a time, composer from Protestant Geneva, he was famously contradictory in his arguments. Rousseau gives us a politics that promises radical individuality while at the same time traps us in the confines of organic community. He seeks to advance humanity toward its natural happiness while accepting and promoting the project of "denaturing" man. He promotes direct democracy yet often falls into totalitarian language. He is a romantic yet at times believes in the supremacy of reason. And he seeks to protect the sovereignty of the inner self while opening it up to manipulation and even, some would argue, disintegration by outside institutions and persons. While I do pay some attention to Rousseau's communitarian sides in this chapter, I emphasize his main object of inquiry at the starting and ending points of his career, the centerpiece of his contribution to the Enlightenment, and the object which future Rousseauist romantic reformers and revolutionaries would later emphasize: the integrity of the inner self in a social world that constantly threatens to colonize it. Since Rousseau's humanistic side is often emphasized in revolutionary language, I emphasize Rousseau's romanticism from his novels and discourses, more so than his formal, constitutionalist writings on the general will. From here, we will be able to differentiate this form of politics from other forms that focus public judgment not on persons, but on disembodied actions in public life.

Rousseau's politics was based on a new and radical metaphysics. Jason Neidleman shows that Rousseau believed that philosophy should not be studied for its own sake, but should take on a moral dimension in the service of human happiness. This stance against the formal, impersonal discipline of philosophy, according to Neidleman, puts Rousseau in the same category as Kierkegaard and Socrates, and firmly against Hegel, Descartes, and other metaphysicians who deal in abstractions. The only way one can begin to search for this kind of moral truth is to examine first and foremost one's relation to oneself. Rather than examining the external world of others, God, or some notion of a well-ordered cosmos, Rousseau urged the self to explore the *sentiment interieur*. This was merely an avenue to this moral truth of human happiness, not an end to the quest for truth itself. Along this journey, one must judge the validity of moral truth based on its utility, autonomy, immediacy, and simplicity. This leads to a number of implications. Moral truth must be *useful* toward the goal of human happiness. The search for moral truth must be guided through examination of one's inner conscience as an outsider apart from the community (since the external world is no reliable source for morality). Moral truth must be discovered through an immediately felt experience rather than based on theory or conjecture dictated by outside forces. And finally, the moral truths realized ought to be simple rather than convoluted or sophisticated.

Abstract philosophies had plagued European society by failing to address important, useful questions. It had allowed room for philosophers to indulge in useless philosophical banter, getting us further away from authentic human happiness.[2] By saying that humans are *naturally* good, Rousseau equates (or, some would say more despairingly, *conflates*) inner truth with moral philosophy.

This radically subjective philosophical stance leads to a politics in which the authentic self is an outsider, equipped to speak honestly from the heart even when among others in physical proximity. The self is governed by the dictates of one's inner conscience rather than by external forces. The politics of authenticity has provided a moral foundation for revolutionaries and reformers to resist injustice and somewhat paradoxically, to join in even more intimate communities with likeminded conscientious objectors who are also occluded. Relatedly, it leads Rousseau to reject the social conventions of the emerging bourgeois public sphere, where men and women speak and act not as authentic selves but as actors playing roles on a public stage. This hostile stance toward social roles has shared much with the identity politics of emancipatory movements ever since, in which the stifling social identities of the oppressed are identified and then overcome through self-realization. We've seen these developments, in which the oppressed join forces to find their collective voice, on both the left and the right in recent years; solidarity based on race, gender, sexual orientation, and class have tended to be staples of the left, though increasingly, these categories are being reorganized and re-conceived, as the right adopts them.

In his plea for the authenticity of modern political actors, Rousseau was railing against what later populists like Andrew Jackson, Betty Friedan, and Donald Trump would: decorum, social roles, and structure which hid or suppressed our natural selves. In his own time, this was manifested in the ruling political structure of the *ancien régime* and the emerging bourgeois public sphere in the social realm that sought to replace it. While the former held individual identities captive behind formal, hierarchical roles held over from the medieval world, the latter created a more fluid world of movement among public actors who performed a multiplicity of roles. But this new form of public action was exercised by individuals still trapped behind performative public masks. While they were different in the way they dispersed authority, the old medieval forms of government and society were similar to emerging modern forms in that individuals were defined by external considerations, whether titles or costumes, rather than by one's unique individuality.

Rousseau finds that when we are defined by external roles, all facets of our civilization are degraded. In his *Discourse on the Arts and Sciences*, he argues that the seeming advancements of civilization that were lauded during the Enlightenment were caused by human vanity rather than creativity and ingenuity. Philosophers, of course, have been making a similar argument for thousands of years (Ecclesiastes famously lamented that "all is vanity"). Yet what was new about Rousseau's critique was that this move from costumed politics to authentic politics had world historical implications, as Rousseau was writing on the cusp of humanity out of one type of political, social, and economic arrangement into another. While ancient and medieval cultures expressed vanity in the costumes of court life and social titles, modern culture expressed vanity through science and commerce. In a striking passage meant to shock self-congratulating Enlightenment philosophes whom Rousseau argues that

[a]stronomy was born out of superstition, eloquence of ambition, hatred, falsehood, and flattery; geometry of avarice; physics of an idle curiosity; all, even moral philosophy, of human pride. Thus the arts and sciences owe their birth to our vices; we should be less doubtful of their advantages, if they had sprung from our virtues.[3]

They not only spring from human vanity, but these modern arts and sciences perpetuate it:

"[a]s the conveniences of life increase, as the arts are brought to perfection, and luxury spreads, true courage flags, military virtues disappear, and all this is the effect of the sciences and of those arts which are exercised in the privacy of men's dwellings."[4]

The rest of European society was celebrating the potential of science and technology to conquer ignorance, want, and material misery that had always plagued humanity. Yet for Rousseau, these modern sciences and arts distract us from our inner selves and, by extension, from each other. What should truly matter to human beings is being true to one's inner self and the public virtues of citizenship that will organically follow from that.

Rousseau's critique of bourgeois society is that psychologically, we have no unique selves, but merely perform, and mimic the performances of others. In his *Letter to M. D'Alembert*, we see Rousseau uses a discussion of theater to make this same point on a political level. As Robert Politzer points out, "Rousseau's discussion of the theatre ... should be interpreted as being simultaneously a discussion of art and society, and of fiction and reality in which the theatre and the actor become the symbols of society and social man."[5] Rousseau expresses his dislike of theater as an art form and of the everyday cultural practice of theatricality more generally. His critique is leveled at two activities: actors performing and audiences watching performances. The regular practice of performing or going to the theater makes hypocrites out of both performers and spectators. He believes that the performances themselves perpetuate the debasement of artistic integrity among actors and artistic appreciation among audiences, alienating both sides. The performing artist merely basks in the applause received from the audience while the audience itself is happy with mediocre works of art that confirm their own substandard tastes and debased morals. "Every artist loves applause," Rousseau regrets. The audience will already have had their tastes corrupted as "the necessary consequence of luxury." From here, the artist "will lower his genius to the level of the age, and will rather submit to compose mediocre works, that will be admired during his lifetime, than labor at sublime achievements which will not be admired till long after he is dead."[6] Spectators identify with and adopt the act of donning a performative mask when they gaze upon these acts. Lionel Trilling says of this impersonation that for Rousseau, "[t]he spectator ... contracts by infection the characteristic disease of the actor, the attenuation of selfhood that results from impersonation."[7]

This apparent dislike of "political theater" extends today to American politics, and the increasing need for candidates to appear authentic and unscripted. This trend perhaps reached its apex at a Wisconsin campaign rally in April of 2016, when presidential candidate Donald Trump told an audience "I can be presidential, but if I was presidential I would only have—about 20 percent of you would be here because it would be boring as hell."[8] While not reaching for sublime rhetorical greatness in this speech, Trump was touching on a long-practiced populist-democratic ideal. He and his supporters, together, were rejecting the social performance in which a president plays the role of president, and the audience reacts with applause for presidential-sounding phrases. In contrast to the more traditional, sober campaign speeches of establishment candidates like Jeb Bush and Marco Rubio, Trump and his audience opted, instead, for the more intimate community that results when people drop their ritualistic performances and act authentically.

Rousseau's critique of the theater held broader political implications than just the erosion of customs and decorum. Rousseau believed that theatrical politics erodes our natural capacity for empathy. By attending theater performances, audiences are able to pretend for a time that they feel for others and identify with their plights. They are able to evade personal responsibility for civic virtue by ventriloquizing pity through actors on a stage. Rousseau thus laments in his *Essay on the Origin of Languages*:

> I have said elsewhere why feigned miseries affect us more than do genuine ones. There are people who sob at tragedies but never in their lives took pity on a single unhappy person. The invention of the theatre is marvelously suited to make our self-love feel proud of all the virtues we do not have.[9]

We see a connection in Rousseau's thought here between the evasion of civic virtue and the debased practice of theatrical playacting. Rousseau was rejecting both the types of public action in which people engaged and the existence of a stage from which this action was performed. He did not wish to see political agency of the self initiated or expressed from a stage, but rather from within. Thus the traditional language of the "political stage" in which citizens are "actors" who perform roles was one Rousseau found troubling since it gave society the ability to evade moral injustices under the surface of public life.

Rousseau took issue not just with stage actors in a theater. The problem of performances was much more socially pervasive. Marshall Berman details how for Rousseau the theatricality of everyday bourgeois public life is a demonstration of performance and modern self-alienation and thus a widespread lack of personal authenticity. In modern Paris, Rousseau's character St. Preux from his novel *Julie* observes, there are many visible acts performed by mobile public actors, but "when a man speaks, it's his costume, not he, that's expressing a feeling." Amid a plethora of public acts, St. Preux sees restless alienated performers "become different from what they are" in order to flatter, impress, or compete with others for stature, wealth, power, or self-worth. Through these activities, any self-worth one gains is relative to what others think of and to one's position above or below them. This is an existential problem that gives modern individuals false consciousness. Although modern individuals believe they have become sovereign individualists, they possess merely public personas and suffer from a "profound passivity underneath" their masks as they define themselves relative to others. In Berman's reading of Rousseau, modern individuals are "just as alienated from themselves as were the aristocrats, peasants, and artisans" of traditional, rural society.[10] For both Rousseau and Berman, the psychic state of the individual had not transformed in the new modern age as it had been promised.

This is how modern men and women lose their senses of self. For Rousseau, the mask donned by the bourgeois allows one to both relate to and compete with others in the political, social, and economic market-places. But as one's motives become tied to those external activities, the individual becomes more alienated from the nature of the inner self and inner motives both multiply and become more malleable. Rousseau laments that the unnatural, externally directed motives of "jealousy, suspicion, fear, coldness, reserve, and hate" are hidden underneath the mask. Theatrical culture "make[s] men double"; there is a silent struggle between their natural potential for goodness and the unnatural public masks they don.[11] Arthur Melzer notes that for Rousseau, the bourgeois is self-alienated because of the psychic disunity this struggle entails. The bourgeois is at peace with neither of his "two lives," which denigrate both the private and public experiences of the self.[12] The bourgeois is somewhere in between, living neither the harmonious, inward existence of natural, pre-social savage in solitude nor the harmonious, outward existence of the citizen acting in public among equals. Worse, this inward world remains unexamined by the modern self, since there are no political or educational mechanisms that could urge introspection.

So what are the characteristics of this presocial, natural self before this split? We get a picture from his *Discourse on the Origin of Inequality*. Here, Rousseau conjectures a state of nature in which man originally existed before the artificial inventions of civil society and government. He attempts to study mankind anthropologically and psychologically. He describes a savage being in nature who can meet one's own physical needs, does not require help or approval from others, and perhaps most importantly for Rousseau's conjecture of man's natural psychology, the savage does not have the faculty of instrumental reason that is used to engage in comparison and competition with others. Rousseau calls this state *amour-propre*, a "self-love" in which one has no need for others because one is perfectly at peace and can survive on one's own.[13] The little relation that savage man has with others is governed by pity, a repugnance to seeing others suffer, which will be important in the development of a moral consciousness once Rousseau prescribes his ideal authentic society later on. Psychologically and spiritually, the savage lives in the moment from within and thus has no need to change one's being in the presence of others. The soul is united into one rather than split, or double. Rousseau paints a romantic picture of the self in this state:

His imagination paints no pictures; his heart makes no demands on him. His few wants are so readily supplied, and he is so far from having the knowledge which is needful to make him want more, that he can have neither foresight nor curiosity. The face of nature becomes indifferent to him as it grows familiar. He sees in it always the same order, the same successions: he has not understanding enough to wonder at the great miracles; nor is it in his mind that we can expect to find that philosophy that man needs, if he is to know how to notice for once what he sees everyday. His soul, which nothing disturbs, is wholly wrapped up in the feeling of its present existence ....[14]

Rousseau here stresses that we are born with a natural self that exists apart from the community. In order to retain its integrity, this self ought not be socially constructed, but it must somehow maintain its sovereignty even amid a fluctuating social and political world. We see here Rousseau's romanticizing of stillness and aloneness in contrast to the dynamism of modern civil society. We see a similar description of the stillness experienced in this sentiment de l'existence in Rousseau's autobiographical *Reveries of a Solitary Walker*. Here, Rousseau's quest for moral truth fulfills the criteria set out in his moral philosophy of utility, autonomy, immediacy, and simplicity:

If there is a state where the soul can find a resting place secure enough to establish itself and concentrate its entire being there, with no need to remember the past or reach into the future, where time is nothing to it, where the present runs on indefinitely but this duration goes unnoticed, with no sign of the passing of time, and no other feeling of deprivation or enjoyment, pleasure or pain, desire or fear than the simple feeling of existence, a feeling that fills our soul entirely, as long as this state lasts, we can call ourselves happy, not with a poor, incomplete, and relative happiness such as we find in the pleasures of life, but with a sufficient complete and perfect happiness which leaves no emptiness to be filled in the soul.[15]

In these two passages Rousseau idealizes solitude over togetherness, stillness over movement, unity over doubleness, and being over appearing.

This distinction between being and appearing is especially pertinent in Rousseau's later prescriptions for intersubjectivity in public life. As mentioned, Rousseau laments the playacting and costume-wearing he saw in modern Parisian society. He loathes it because it "make[s] men double." In our natural state, Rousseau conjectures, "men found their security in how easily they saw through one another" when "outer appearances were always the likeness of the heart's dispositions."[16] Today, we might describe this state as a politician "saying what they mean." Once savage man left the parasitic state of nature, he entered a state in which "one had to seem other than one in fact was. To be and to appear became two entirely different things, and from this distinction arose ostentatious display, deceitful cunning, and all the vices that follow in their wake."[17] With the entrance of civil society comes the development of opacity among individuals and thus a lack of trust.

Rousseau's task becomes to ensure that the modern individual can develop and maintain their authenticity intact in a fallen world. In order to understand how the politics of authenticity sees the self in relation to society and politics, we need to examine how this moral development is cultivated by Rousseau in a dialectical way through education and through governmental institutions. We need to note three important considerations that allow Rousseau to reconcile his ideal of presocial individuality with the irreversible fact that human beings came to live in collectivities. These are the ways in which he is able to shift from imagining nature to imagining a good society that encompasses the best parts of nature. Firstly, Rousseau admits that his version of the state of nature should not be taken as an absolute and that it would, in fact, be impossible to know exactly what the original condition of human beings was before civil society and government:

> Like the statue of Glaucus, which was so disfigured by time, seas, and tempests, that it looked more like a wild beast than a god, the human soul, altered in society by a thousand causes perpetually recurring, by the acquisition of a multitude of truths and errors, by the changes happening to the constitution of the body, and by the continual jarring of the passions, has, so to speak, changed in appearance, so as to be hardly recognizable. Instead of a being, acting constantly from fixed and invariable principles, instead of that celestial and majestic simplicity, impressed on it by its divine Author, we find it only the frightful contrast of passion mistaking itself for reason, and of understanding grown delirious.[18]

Rousseau also admits that in attempting to describe mankind's original nature, he may have "involuntarily put in something of my own."[19] Thus, Rousseau is telling us that human nature itself is alterable. Secondly, Rousseau needs to account for the fact that we cannot go back to nature in a perfect sense. The savage man that he idealizes ultimately falls from grace once the wicked artifice of reason, the presence of other persons, and thus a competitive spirit (which corresponds to bourgeois notions of private property) take hold.[20] The civilized individual begins accumulating material goods and needs more and more. This creates an imbalance between one's wants and one's ability to satisfy those wants which quickly become needs. A society is then created to provide for those needs. Individuals lose their naturalness by surrounding themselves with artifice that brings their attention out of themselves. Reforming the self, society, and government needs to take this new reality into consideration as it moves forward.

Thirdly, as Guignon notes, Rousseau is especially powerful in his ability to imagine radically new political communities because he never quite belonged to any nation. He is well equipped to speak in relativistic terms in his autobiographical works, since his self-analysis does not correspond to any political or linguistic perspective.[21] Similar to subsequent reformers and revolutionaries who are oppressed or occluded from the political system, their only recourse is to argue from personal experience rather than to the history or traditions of the nation. This outsider perspective affords them an authoritative voice, because they do not hold the same national or ideological baggage as do those who are enfranchised by the system. In the United States, as faith in institutional politics has eroded, we've seen this outsider phenomenon manifest in nearly every successful presidential candidate since the 1970s.

Lastly and most importantly, like for Kant, as well as social reformers throughout modernity, Rousseau overcomes the tension between self and society through the metaphysical idea that one can acquire universal moral truths about humanity through radical introspection. In *On Being Authentic*, Charles Guignon points out that for Rousseau "[t]he turn inward is supposed to lead us to a dimension of the self that transcends our particularity. It is deep within myself that I find I am part of Nature or The World Spirit or Humankind or the realm of imagination, creativity and beauty."[22] According to Charles Taylor, what is "modern" about the universality of the truths discovered through this introspection is that the inner voice is some conception of nature and not necessarily God.[23] Whereas Christians had concluded that humans were children of God by contemplating the truths of scripture, Rousseau and other humanists concluded that they were children of *nature*, by contemplating the truths of themselves.

This type of inward turn differentiates Rousseau from other modern thinkers in how he thinks about the self, society, and what introspection can tell us about moral universal political principles. Taylor notes that Locke, Descartes, and other bourgeois liberal rationalists despised by Rousseau see reason as the governing principle of the "punctual self." A number of implications stem from this rationalist principle. The self is seen as a *tabula rasa* with no preexisting inner content, shaped only by external environmental forces. Therefore, far from finding "the moral law within" to use the language of Kant (or the "savage" man within, to paraphrase Rousseau), one finds nothing moral within oneself to explore. Self-knowledge becomes a scientific process of disengaging and objectifying oneself from a distance in order to understand and then control one's thinking and behavior. At the individual level, this disengaged reason, for Rousseau, alienates us from our natural, moral, spiritual unity and splits us into two. As Taylor notes, this creates the "central place of the disengaged, disciplinary stance to the self in our culture."[24] This feeling of disengagement and seeing oneself and others as morally neutral allows us to navigate a modern capitalist society. Just as we have emptied and split ourselves, we empty others as well of their moral content, split from them, and then are forced to consider ways to control, compete with, and often manipulate them. At the social level, disengaged reason prevents us from knowing each other in an honest and intimate way since we understand that all is surface, and that there is no moral content behind the masks of others we encounter in public life.

In contrast to disengaged reason and the *tabula rasa*, Rousseau has vision of "conscience" within. This conscience has the power to morally transform our will while also allowing us to see the moral transformations of others. But we need to directly experience the relation of ourselves *to* ourselves without rational detachment. As Jean Starobinski says of Rousseau's impact, "we have moved from the realm of (historical) truth to that of authenticity."[25] We move from an objective view of the self endorsed by rational self-detachment, and toward a subjective view of the self celebrated by the Rousseauists. We can then overcome our detachment from others; the psychic disengagement we have from them would collapse if individuals spoke to one another from the heart rather than speaking from a costume and merely acknowledging others' costumes.

Rousseau's writings idealize a complete and autonomous soul in solitude, yet in order to acknowledge the impossibility of going back to prelapsarian nature (or even knowing precisely what it is), Rousseau must detail how to create the autonomous citizen throughout one's educational development in real time. Progress requires the transformation of the human will away from the vanities that resulted from savage man's self-alienating fall, which was unguided, and toward the development of individual moral conscience, which should be guided. This project is most systematically outlined in his educational novel *Emile*. Rousseau's teleology here is to demonstrate how to educate a child from birth to adulthood so that one's intellectual and physical development will be an unfolding of one's unique individuality. He will then explore how to protect and promote that individuality once one becomes an adult citizen.

He begins by insisting that children ought to be shielded from public opinion so that one discovers one's own authentic self in solitude before joining with others. Developing the self without interference from public opinion and with the aid of a tutor, Rousseau's pupil Emile is guided through experiences that create an equilibrium between his will and his power to achieve his will, an equilibrium which may have existed for savage man, but is always out of balance in bourgeois society. Having struck this equilibrium, Emile learns rationally (as savage man intuitively knew) that "he is always master of himself."[26] The approximation of the natural sentiment of existence makes the individual authentic and "truly one" rather than split between his inner potential for individuality and the external, publicly defined mask. It gives Emile "consciousness of the self" that makes him need "recourse to others less frequently."[27]

But the unified self is always in danger of disintegration upon contact with others. Like all individuals, Emile has a proclivity to leave his natural, autonomous state and hand control of his selfhood over to others. The task of the tutor is to supply Emile with an agency that will unite him with others in such a way that preserves and enhances his authenticity rather than destroying it. This faculty is compassion or conscience, which approximates the pitié of presocial, natural man. In the amoral state of nature, pitié was a *negative* instinct, serving as a buffer between individuals and preventing anyone from desiring to harm anyone else, thus keeping each individual in solitude. But since individuals in society must be more active in their dealings with others, the passiveness of pitié must be transformed into active compassion, a moral faculty that one exercises toward others. Compassion stems from the recognition of the "moral order" of society by the inner conscience and manifests outwardly in social commiseration. As Laurence Cooper demonstrates, Rousseau's compassion is meant to replace the alienating motivations of envy, mimicry, and competition as the modes of interaction between individuals.[28] Although compassion is the foundation of intimate community, its ultimate function for Rousseau is to protect the autonomy of the individual who possesses it. This newly created individual, with the capacity for a radically individualistic autonomy as well as the capacity for intimate compassion, will be required for the social contract to hold.

Rousseau has the seemingly impossible task, then, of imagining a government that is just while also assuming that it grows organically out of civil society in which much injustice already exists. An equally daunting task is imagining a government which respects the authenticity of individuals while also creating an organic collectivity. If we are to maintain Rousseau's own assertion that his writings taken together created an "interconnected system" with only trivial contradictions, then we must attempt to see *The Social Contract* as a text which addresses and perhaps achieves both of these tasks in lights of his other writings.

Is Rousseau attempting to recover nature for mankind or to create citizens? Was Rousseau merely romanticizing a return of human beings back into beasts in a state of nature or does his political theory abandon the idealist anchor of nature and move instead to the realist task of constructing an artificial political order? The answers to these questions are ambiguous. On the one hand, as he says in *Emile*, one cannot be man and citizen at the same time and thus his job is to denature man. Yet in *The Social Contract*, Rousseau says in several passages that the new political society he is constructing will be founded on nature. The great paradox of *The Social Contract*, as William Bluhm notes, is that Rousseau "did denature man, and yet he did found his state on human nature."[29] We can say that by creating a dialectic between autonomy in a pre-political state of nature and community in a civil state, Rousseau was attempting to bring human beings forward toward a happier, more just state of authenticity and self-rule in which nature is achieved rather than recovered.

In *The Social Contract*, Rousseau has two seemingly contradictory projects. One deals not with freedom but with legitimacy. Here, he abandons his romantic idealism of reproducing free and natural man and attempts instead to make mankind's chains "legitimate."[30] Yet while he does alter his reverence for natural freedom, he does not abandon it. In addition to legitimizing chains, his goal is to advance the project of autonomy for the individual where "each, while uniting himself with all, may still obey himself alone, and remain as free as before." The social contract that Rousseau stipulates "follow[s] from the nature of things."[31] Clearly he is not referring to the nature of perfect stillness experienced by himself in his *Confessions* nor of the savage in his *Origins*, but a nature that is unfolding as humanity progresses; in other words, this is the same type of unfolding of "nature" through time, development, and guidance that his pupil Emile experiences. As he is led to improve his moral condition as he moves through stages of his own development, so too can humanity. Thus while nature is not as static here and is a more fluid concept than it is in Rousseau's romantic writings, it still grounds him in an ideal to be achieved. What allows Rousseau the room to alter his earlier more static view of prelapsarian nature is his belief in the transformation of the individual will away from avarice (as savage man experienced without guidance) and toward virtue (as Emile experienced with guidance). On this point, we see as central Rousseau's theory of the general will, the requirement of guidance from a wise public educator known as "the Lawgiver." While Rousseau leaves the description of this figure or office ambiguous, he does say that this guiding hand will have to come from outside the community or prior to the social contract. The lawmaker, much like the tutor in Emile, will give to the people the proper moral code that will make it possible for them to exhibit the sorts of civic virtue necessary in a direct democracy.

Further, Rousseau alters his vision of nature not only based on the impact of education, but also of the suprahuman force of history that can resolve certain dialectical tensions. Rousseau's messianic view saw the movement toward democracy as inevitable. The use of calculating reason that Rousseau saw and lamented in bourgeois society, once combined with the public value of authentic expression, will lead to emancipation. Charles Taylor describes romanticism's view of history as "growth through a spiral, moving in the end towards a reconciliation of reason and feeling."[32] The "spiraling" of these two opposing human faculties will lead to a celebratory democracy for Rousseau that values both compassion stemming from within individuals, and collective intimacy that will break down the opaque barriers outside of and in between individuals. This belief that history is bending in the direction of progress, extending freedom, democracy, and happiness to more and more people, is a part of Enlightenment thinking that frequently animates movements for justice.

In addition to expressing and protecting individual authenticity, compassion creates an intimate community as a corrective to the vain egoism of bourgeois theatrical culture. Rousseau's *Letter to M. D'Alembert on the Theatre* promotes a celebratory, participatory politics for republics in which authentic, unmasked autonomous actors, equipped with compassion from within, "assemble often" in the "festive air" and are brought together by "sweet bonds of pleasure and joy."[33] Marshall Berman argues that this celebratory compassion is meant to "bring people together in a new way through festivals of democracy" which will "set a vision of a spontaneous festival, in the open air ... bringing all the people together, embodying and expressing their freedom."[34] Berman goes on to celebrate that in this participatory democracy, the people themselves are to be "the object of these entertainments" rather than being divided between actors and spectators.[35] Charles Taylor notes that Rousseau's "good political community is bound together by a sentiment which is an extension of the joy that humans feel in each others' company, even in the most ordinary and intimate contexts."[36] Making spectators part of the performance itself has been central to many democratic movements throughout modernity. In the festival-like rallies of Donald Trump, the audience itself seemed to become a character in the act. This idea of the audience being part of the performance was reflected in one of Barack Obama's 2008 mantras that "we are the change we've been waiting for."

As Frederick Barnard argues, Rousseau's ideal of patriotic citizenship unites individuals around the public expression of sentiment rather than their use of instrumental reason.[37] Rousseau believes that sentiment better approximates man's natural authentic freedom than does reason. Patriotic citizenship stems from sentimental expression, which is natural to human beings. The coupling of one's natural traits with the traits necessary for patriotic citizenship is what can make the new modern citizen "truly one." The natural, private self is being reconciled and combined with the political, public self. Unlike in societies in which there was a strict division between private and public life, to be patriotic in a Rousseauist polity is to have undivided loyalties between the self and the nation. Those who demonstrate this indivisibility are deemed authentic, rustic, simple, uncorrupted, much like Rousseau's pre-political savage. We saw this exhibited most explicitly in the populist vice presidential run of Sarah Palin in 2008, when she praised her audience as being citizens of "real America."[38]

Notoriously, for Rousseau, the creation of these authentic subjects does first involve political coercion, just as education of the pupil in his *Emile* requires coercion by the tutor. Indeed, Rousseau famously declares in *The Social Contract* that those who do not voluntarily contract with the community must be "forced to be free."[39] As it turns out, returning to "nature" involves many unnatural mechanisms (this is a point to which we will return when we discuss Arendt's analysis of the Jacobins in the next chapter). Nevertheless, Rousseau's aim in collapsing the categories of private authenticity and public freedom is to create a society where the individual remains "as free as before" he or she contracted with others. Rousseau's exploration of the human heart has had the lingering effect of shifting politics away from the public words and deeds of men and women and into their private intentions and sentiments. The private realm, for Rousseau and his romantic brethren, became political. In the end, this project begins and ends with the self. In the romantic ideal, we do not develop a moral conscience by adhering to the artificiality of external, impersonal laws meant to denaturalize us. Governance then becomes about

> transforming each individual, who is by himself a complete and solitary whole, into part of a greater whole from which he in a manner receives his life and being; of altering man's constitution for the purpose of strengthening it; and of substituting a partial and moral existence for the physical and independent existence nature has conferred on us all.[40]

Thus, democratic governance both springs from the discovery of natural moral conscience one discovers from introspective self-development, and then is reinforced in public life among other authentic citizens.

The politics of authenticity that Rousseau systematized is reflective of populist, democratic movements before, during, and after the Enlightenment. These movements promise to emancipate their followers from some artificial, external threat. There are certain variations between different writers and activists that emphasize different parts of the Rousseauist paradigm when arguing for authenticity. One variation of authentic politics emphasizes the recourse to private introspection to make a political argument about the larger social-political world. Another variant emphasizes not only spiritual introspection about oneself, but the perspective of the lived experience of oppression or occlusion. And lastly, we see among many proponents of authenticity a call for democratic solidarity and identity politics to challenge oppression behind the closed doors of private spaces. What these variations share is a propensity for unmasked, moral truth-telling in the public sphere.

Rousseau's dedication to public truth-telling serves as a vital fulcrum in the history of authenticity. Historically and conceptually, Rousseau stands on the cusp of ancient and medieval sources of moral truth, which are theistic, and modern sources of truth which are secular, but still often employ otherworldly sources of truth. In these ways, Rousseauist truth-telling could be described as *prophetic*. In prophesy, the truth is discovered by reference to an otherworldly realm of being, outside the space of appearance. Often, the telling of prophesy requires an attention to an inner, spiritual reality, since the concrete world of others is corrupt. Socrates, for example, shuns performance and speaks truth to the Athenian jury based on reference to the mystic Oracle of Delphi.[41] He tells this prophetic truth without fear of death of the body, because truth exists outside the physical world. Luther came to the door of the church in Wittenberg, facing the prospect of persecution, yet armed with the otherworldly and introspective truth that "it is not by works but by faith alone that man is saved."

Because truth is reached through introspection rather than a thorough understanding of a complex, plural social world, its telling is often direct and unfiltered. Telling the truth can be, as George Orwell says, a revolutionary act. Jacobins believed in the eventual transformation of the human will toward a republic of virtue, where truth was to be spoken transparently, publicly, and without veils. As Marisa Linton notes: "Revolutionary politics were constructed against old regime politics, and characterized in terms of polarities: virtue and corruption, transparency and secrecy authenticity and duplicity."[42] We also see this in radical American revolutionaries like Thomas Paine, who used the legitimizing force of nature to argue for an uncovering of the oppressive veil with which England claimed dominion over the American colonies. Of English Kings, Paine wrote "could we take off the dark covering of antiquity and trace them to their first rise, we should find the first of them nothing better than the principal ruffian of some restless gang." Instead of keeping citizens separate from each other and from their government, Paine argues, "society promotes our happiness positively by uniting our affections." Paine was able to reach this truth through a radically subjectivist turn: "my own line of reasoning is to myself as straight and clear as a ray of light."[43] In his essay "The Democratization of Mind in the American Revolution," Gordon Wood argues that Paine's writing style *Common Sense* broke away from the gentlemanly literary and rhetorical customs of the day in its frankness, sincerity, and populism:

> [*Common Sense*] broke through the presuppositions of politics and offered new ways of conceiving of government that had not been said before. But some of the awe and consternation the pamphlet aroused came from its deliberate elimination of the usual elitist apparatus of persuasion and its

acknowledged appeal to a wider reading public. Paine's arguments are sometimes tortured, and the logic is often deficient. There are few of the traditional gentlemanly references to learned authorities … Paine scorned 'words of sound' that only 'amuse the ear' and relied on a simple and direct idiom; he used concrete, even course and vulgar, imagery drawn from the commonplace world that could be understood even by the unlearned.[44]

Paine—as is common with the more radical revolutionaries in both America and beyond—rejected the formalities and costumes of politics and the written argument (this rejection of formality would be reversed in some ways by the more elitist authors of the American Constitution and especially *The Federalist Papers*, which reject the revolutionary attitudes of the 1770s).

Since the late eighteenth century, other revolutionaries have emphasized the importance of discovering truth from introspection rather than from a careful examination of external, political considerations. Karl Marx might be the most consequential example of this. For Marx's revolution to become reality, like for Rousseau he requires that workers overcome their "false consciousness" that they were free when in fact they were not. Like other revolutionaries, he then urges individuals to unite under the unitary identity of "workers," rather than under a multiplicity of identities that modern society affixes to us.[45] This radical self-realization will then extend to communal identity. The process of realizing that one is defined, exclusively, as part of a group has been part of mass movements, social movements, and, today, identity politics, throughout modernity. Marshall Berman shows how Marx argued that the material misery of the proletariat can be transcended through Rousseauist politics. In reaction to modernity's "icy water of egoistical calculation,"

> workers can come through the affliction and the fear only by making contact with the self's deepest resources … they will be prepared to fight for collective recognition of the self's beauty and value. Their communism, when it comes, will appear as a kind of transparent garment, at once keeping its wearers warm and setting off their naked beauty, so that they can recognize themselves and each other in all their radiance.[46]

Revolution by introspection was not just a class-based phenomenon. For nineteenth-century thinkers who imagined radically different societies, change started with introspection. We can see further examples of authenticity at work in the emerging intellectual movements of Jacksonian America. The New England Transcendentalists attempted to radicalize education and social life in a way Rousseau would have admired. These reforms were in reaction to the rising liberal instrumentalism and the corrupting influence of commercial society on the self. In 1842, Elizabeth Palmer Peabody wrote "Plan of the West Roxbury Community" in *The Dial*, a Transcendentalist newsletter, which described the purposes of Brook Farm, a new experimental commune outside of Boston. She explained that the community allowed its members "leisure to live in all the faculties of the soul" rather than in the dictates of the marketplace. Amos Bronson Alcott and other Transcendentalists sought to revolutionize childhood education based on radical subjective principles which, while they were more theistic, were similar to those in Rousseau's *Emile*. According to Philip Gura,

> [The Transcendentalists], excited by the idea that everyone, from birth, possessed a divine element, altered long-established pedagogy to cultivate this divine essence. They sought to replace Locke's influential psychological paradigm—which posits the mind of each child at birth as a tabula rasa, or a blank slate, upon which sensory experience writes its lessons—with the idealist notion that the mind has innate principles, including the religious sentiment, a view of education that requires a different pedagogy. The teacher has to help each child recognize and cultivate his internal principles. The classroom no longer was a place of rote learning, but an arena where even very young students were taught to cultivate heightened self-consciousness.[47]

Gura goes on to describe how the new classroom contained "movable desks so that the center of the room was open for group activities" and how Alcott "varied the day's work with nature walks, physical exercises, storytelling, and directed conversation."[48] Even at the university level this belief in the innate faculties of students held for the Transcendentalists. Ralph Waldo Emerson gave a graduation speech that shocked the faculty of Harvard Divinity School (and had him banned for two decades) in which he proclaimed that

> The intuition of the moral sentiment is an insight of the perfection of the laws of the soul. These laws execute themselves. They are out of time, out of space, and not subject to circumstance. Thus; in the soul of man there is a justice whose retributions are instant and entire.

Based on this tenet, he went on to rail against

[t]he stationariness of religion; the assumption that the age of inspiration is
past, that the Bible is closed; the fear of degrading the character of Jesus by
representing him as a man; indicate with sufficient clearness the falsehood of
our theology.[49]

We see this same sort of democratization today: lived experience is much
more valid and recognizable than traditions or institutions.

Those who wrote and argued authenticity made more direct political
appeals in Jacksonian America. Another Transcendentalist fellow traveler,
Orestes Brownson, predating *The Communist Manifesto* by eight years,
spoke from the perspective of the occluded in the emerging factories. He
argued that if one looks at the world from the perspective of "the actual
condition of the laboring classes, viewed simply and exclusively in their
capacity as laborers, one would see "wage slavery" denied individuals their
dignity and indeed was even worse than chattel slavery.[50] Neo-feudalist,
anti-democrats of the south like George Fitzhugh made similar arguments, but from the perspective of one who did not wish to undo the
socially stratified nature of southern life.[51]

Political focus shifted from the external to the internal realm, and from
formal politics to social issues. The rise of the novel in the nineteenth century signals part of this development. But autobiography, especially, came to
rival political science in legitimacy when it came to investigating and ques-
tioning laws and institutions. In gory detail, Frederick Douglass describes
his personal experience in great detail in *Narrative of the Life of Frederick
Douglass, an American Slave*, to shed light on the institution of slavery, a
previously "private" institution whose practices were considered to be
largely beyond the reach of governmental regulation or public awareness.[52]
Douglass's struggles become the struggles of a race. Elizabeth Cady Stanton
argues for constitutional rights for women from her own perspective of
occlusion in the private domestic sphere, another realm considered to be
private and apolitical. She injects the personal into the political by adopting
the universalist, revolutionary rhetoric of the Declaration of Independence.
In it, she lists the grievances she faces in her lived experience:

He has never permitted her to exercise her inalienable right to the elective
franchise. He has compelled her to submit to laws, in the formation of which
she had no voice. He has withheld from her rights which are given to the

most ignorant and degraded men-both natives and foreigners. Having deprived her of this first right of a citizen, the elective franchise, thereby leaving her without representation in the halls of legislation, he has oppressed her on all sides. He has made her, if married, in the eye of the law, civilly dead. He has taken from her all right in property, even to the wages she earns.[53]

In another piece by Stanton, she, like Rousseau, argues for individual rights based on the modern reality of solitude in everyday life and the natural right to self-determination that governments must protect:

The strongest reason for giving woman all the opportunities for higher education, for the full development of her faculties, her forces of mind and body; for giving her the most enlarged freedom of thought and action; a complete emancipation from all forms of bondage, of custom, dependence, superstition; from all the crippling influences of fear—is the solitude and personal responsibility of her own individual life. The strongest reason why we ask for woman a voice in the government under which she lives; in the religion she is asked to believe; equality in social life, where she is the chief factor; a place in the trades and professions, where she may earn her bread, is because of her birthright to self-sovereignty; because, as an individual, she must rely on herself. No matter how much women prefer to lean, to be protected and supported, nor how much men desire to have them do so, they must make the voyage of life alone, and for safety in an emergency, they must know something of the laws of navigation. To guide our own craft, we must be captain, pilot, engineer; with chart and compass to stand at the wheel; to watch the winds and waves, and know when to take in the sail, and to read the signs in the firmament over all. It matters not whether the solitary voyager is man or woman; nature, having endowed them equally, leaves them to their own skill and judgment in the hour of danger, and, if not equal to the occasion, alike they perish.[54]

Since these budding social movements of the Jacksonian Era, the twentieth century yielded a number of authentic political actors, most notably activists in the Civil Rights and feminist movements. It also saw reactions to the spiritually deadening and often oppressive mechanisms of modernity in which the self, while more materially comfortable, was corrupted and disoriented with anomie. The Frankfurt School produced a number of texts challenging the ideologies and practices of the late modern bourgeois public sphere that colonize the self and destroy individuality. Echoing Rousseau's lament of artistic mediocrity in his *Letter to M. D'Alembert*, Horkheimer and Adorno rail against the "culture industry" for transforming the potentially emancipatory practice of artistic expression into mere capitalist profit. The 1950s and 1960s produced a number of screeds against the complacency and conformity of postwar America.

While the merging of the personal with the political has led to great emancipatory movements, some argue that it has also led to a stifling authoritarian impulse and mob mentality. George Kateb argues that Rousseau's direct democracy, far from promoting and protecting individual freedom, spells a great loss for individuality. Kateb believes that in the modern world, a moderate amount of groundlessness and anomie go hand in hand with individuality. This combination of groundlessness and individuality is best protected by a representative democracy that keeps a proper opacity between citizens and between citizens and their government. As a proto-totalitarian community, Rousseau's direct democracy solves too many questions with too many simple answers. Rousseau's community is, Kateb notes, "small, simple, and static." There can be "no individuality." Rousseau's community is:

> a great moral vision; but the loss to humanity, the loss in humanity, is unspeakably great. The raw materials of the modern self are removed from community. Not enough of its necessities are accommodated: distance between people … the sense that the world is a strange place. Moderate alienation and moderate anomie are extinguished. The preconditions of the dispositions sponsored by representative democracy are enfeebled. The Rousseauist community discourages independence of spirit and the sense of moral indeterminacy.[55]

This lack of distance between citizens and their government in a direct democracy, Kateb argues, makes it more difficult for citizens to protest, since it makes "any impulse to dissent into an act of shameful rebellion against oneself."[56] Adding to the chorus of lamentations over transparent and direct democracy were writers of the twentieth century who saw in Rousseau the loss of individual freedom and, at worse, full-scale totalitarianism. Isaiah Berlin, in particular, argued that Rousseau "claims to have been the most ardent and passionate lover of human liberty whoever lived" but yet was "one of the most sinister and formidable enemies of liberty in the whole history of modern thought."[57]

We see then that from both intellectual and political corners, projects for democratic emancipation of the self and of private spaces in general have faced a backlash. Philosophically, the backlash is based on the belief that in order for representative democracy to thrive, there must be mechanisms that create buffers between citizens in their private spheres. This view tends to see politics as agonal, where public life is and ought to be an arena for performance over expression, opacity over transparency, and self-interest over public interest; we ought to wear masks in public rather than "be ourselves." Politically from the anti-democratic right, elites have sought to prevent the personal from becoming political so that domination can continue unchecked in what are traditionally considered to be private spaces. Yet this permeability between private and public also alarms postmodern democrats on the left. This is the fear that the politicization of identity leads to the colonization of the self from elites. In the next chapter, I expand on the backlash against authenticity from the perspective of Hannah Arendt, whose political theory has been utilized philosophically and politically by both the right and the postmodern left as an alternative to the politics of authenticity.

Both sides of the ideological spectrum have railed against the excesses of authenticity in full force since the 1960s. At the same time, there have been few academic or political voices since then arguing for the idea that authenticity is even a worthy discourse to consider in addressing our social and political problems. Ironically, this is precisely because we are so inundated with claims of authenticity from advertising, political campaigns, social media, and, now, the presidency that we fail to notice it as a revolutionary idea. It is so pervasive in our culture that we hardly notice its power. As Thomas Frank argues in *The Conquest of Cool*, late capitalism saw the complete co-opting of the discourse by the forces against which the discourse used to rail.[58] The popularization of Mao and Che Guevara T-shirts proves this; in an ironic counter-attack on communization of revolution, a popular T-shirt arose recently with a picture of Che with the text "I don't actually know who this is." It is precisely in the moment when we are least aware of this co-opting and most subjected to the colonization of the self that the discourse (even if modified by some elements of performative politics) is most needed.

NOTES

1. Nelson Lund, "Jean-Jacques Rousseau: Not a Nut, Not a Leftist, Not an Irresponsible Intellectual," *The Washington Post*, January 2, 2017, https://www.washingtonpost.com/news/volokh-conspiracy/wp/2017/01/02/jean-jacques-rousseau-not-a-nut-not-a-leftist-and-not-an-irresponsible-intellectual/.
2. Jason Neidleman, "The Sublime Science of Simple Souls: Rousseau's Philosophy of Truth," *History of European Ideas* 39, no. 6 (2013): 815–34.

3. Jean-Jacques Rousseau, "*A Discourse on the Arts and Sciences*" in *The Social Contract and Discourses*, trans. G.D.H Cole (London: J.M. Dent, 1993), 62.
4. Rousseau, *Arts and Sciences*, 20.
5. Robert L. Politzer, "Rousseau on the Theatre and the Actors," *Romanic Review* 46 (1955): 250–57.
6. Rousseau, *Arts and Sciences*, 19.
7. Lionel Trilling, *Sincerity and Authenticity* (Cambridge, MA: Harvard UP, 1972), 69–70.
8. Nolan D McCaskill, "Trump: Acting More Presidential Would be Boring as Hell," *Politico*, April 4, 2016, https://www.politico.com/blogs/2016-gop-primary-live-updates-and-results/2016/04/donald-trump-act-presidential-boring-as-hell-221546.
9. Jean-Jacques Rousseau, and Johann Gottfried Herder, *On the Origin of Language*, ed. Moran, John H. and Alexander Gode (Chicago: University of Chicago Press, 1986), 8.
10. Marshall Berman, *The Politics of Authenticity: Radical Individualism and the Emergence of Modern Society* (London: Verso, 2009), 115–16.
11. Rousseau, *Arts and Sciences*, 7.
12. Arthur Melzer, "Rousseau and the Problem of Bourgeois Society," *American Political Science Review* 74.4 (1980), 1031.
13. Jean-Jacques Rousseau, "A Discourse on the Origin of Inequality" in *The Social Contract and Discourses*, trans. G.D.H Cole (London: J.M. Dent, 1993), 43.
14. Rousseau, *Origin of Inequality*, 62.
15. Jean-Jacques Rousseau, *Reveries of a Solitary Walker*, trans. Charles E. Butterworth (Indianapolis, IN: Hackett Pub., 1992), 68–69.
16. Rousseau, *Origin of Inequality*, 6.
17. Rousseau, *Origin of Inequality*, 95.
18. Rousseau, *Origin of Inequality*, 42.
19. Rousseau, *Origin of Inequality*, 51.
20. Rousseau, *Origin of Inequality*, 62.
21. Charles B. Guignon, *On Being Authentic* (London: Routledge, 2004), 67.
22. Guignon, *On Being Authentic*, 67.
23. Charles Taylor, *Sources of the Self: The Making of the Modern Identity* (Cambridge, MA: Harvard UP, 1989), 366.
24. Taylor, *Sources of the Self*, 175.
25. Jean Starobinski, *Jean-Jacques Rousseau: Transparency and Obstruction*, trans. Arthur Goldhammer (Chicago and London, 1988), 197.
26. Jean-Jacques Rousseau, *Emile*, trans. Allan Bloom. (London: J.M. Dent, 1993), 40.
27. Rousseau, *Emile*, 161.

28. Laurence D. Cooper, *Rousseau, Nature, and the Problem of the Good Life* (University Park, PA: Pennsylvania State UP, 1999), 98–100.
29. William T. Bluhm, "Freedom in the Social Contract: Rousseau's Legitimate Chains," *Polity* 16, no. 3 (1984): 363.
30. Rousseau, *Origin of Inequality*, 181.
31. *Origin of Inequality*, 190.
32. Charles Taylor. *Sources of the Self*, 366.
33. Jean-Jacques Rousseau and Jean Le Rond D'Alembert, *Politics and the Arts; Letter to M. D'Alembert on the Theatre* (Ithaca, NY: Cornell University Press, 1968), 125.
34. Berman, *The Politics of Authenticity*, xii.
35. Berman, *The Politics of Authenticity*, 215.
36. Taylor, *Sources of the Self*, 366.
37. Frederick Barnard, "Patriotism and Citizenship in Rousseau: A Dual Theory of Public Willing?," *The Review of Politics* 46, no. 2 (1984): 244.
38. Mark Leibovich, "Palin Visits a 'Pro-America' Kind of Town," *The New York Times*, October 17, 2008, https://thecaucus.blogs.nytimes.com/2008/10/17/palin-visits-a-pro-america-kind-of-town/.
39. Jean-Jacques Rousseau, "*The Social Contract*" in *The Social Contract And Discourses*, trans. G.D.H Cole (London: J.M. Dent, 1993), 195.
40. Rousseau, "*The Social Contract*," 214.
41. see Plato *The Trial and Death of Socrates: Euthyphro, Apology, Crito, Death Scene from Phaedo*, G. M. A. Grube, and John M. Cooper (Indianapolis, IN: Hackett Pub., 2000).
42. Marisa Linton, *Choosing Terror: Virtue, Friendship and Authenticity in the French Revolution* (Oxford: Oxford University Press, 2013), 285.
43. Thomas Paine, "Common Sense" in *American Political Thought: A Norton Anthology*. ed. Isaac Kramnick and Theodore J. Lowi (New York: W.W. Norton, 2009), 131.
44. Gordon Wood, "The Democratization of Mind in the American Revolution" in *The Moral Foundations of the American Republic*, ed. Robert H. Horwitz (Charlottesville: University Press of Virginia, 1986), 117–18.
45. see Karl Marx and Friedrich Engels, "Manifesto of the Communist Party," in *The Marx-Engels Reader*, ed. Robert C. Tucker (New York: Norton, 1978), 469.
46. Berman, *All That Is Solid Melts into Air*, 110.
47. Philip F. Gura, *American Transcendentalism: A History* (New York: Hill and Wang, 2007), 159.
48. Gura, *American Transcendentalism*, 84.
49. Ralph Waldo Emerson, "The Divinity School Address" in *The Essential Writings of Ralph Waldo Emerson* (New York: Modern Library, 2000), 64.

50. See Orestes Augustus Brownson, *The Laboring Classes: An Article from the Boston Quarterly Review* (Boston: B.H. Greene, 1840).

51. See George Fitzhugh, *Cannibals All! Or, Slaves without Masters* (Cambridge: Belknap Press of Harvard University Press, 1960).

52. See Frederick Douglass, *Narrative of the Life of Frederick Douglass, an American Slave*, ed. David W. Blight (Boston: Bedford Books of St. Martin's Press, 1993).

53. Elizabeth Cady Stanton, "The Seneca Falls Declaration of Sentiments and Resolutions" in *American Political Thought: A Norton Anthology*, ed. Isaac Kramnick and Theodore J. Lowi (New York: W.W. Norton, 2009), 530.

54. Elizabeth Cady Stanton, *Solitude of Self* (Ashfield, MA: Paris Press, 2001), 7.

55. George Kateb, *The Inner Ocean: Individualism and Democratic Culture* (Ithaca, NY: Cornell UP), 1992, 55.

56. Kateb, *Inner Ocean*, 55.

57. Isaiah Berlin, *Freedom and Its Betrayal: Six Enemies of Human Liberty* (Princeton, NJ: Princeton University Press, 2002), 52.

58. Thomas Frank. *The Conquest of Cool: Business Culture, Counterculture, and the Rise of Hip Consumerism* (Chicago: U of Chicago, 1997).

CHAPTER 3

The Politics of Theatricality

Is meaningful, effective political action possible without an authentic identity recognized by oneself and others? After surveying the landscape of
Rousseauist political action in the last chapter, we can determine that for
Rousseau and those he influenced, the answer is no. The purposes of the
authentic political life relate both to the integrity of the self and to justice
in the political sphere. This leads to two types of "uncovering" that take
place. Firstly, modern individuals remove their public masks and assert
their private experiences into public deliberation. Secondly, the public itself
unearths and rights moral wrongs that were heretofore hidden from public
scrutiny in private spaces. In these ways, Rousseau and the other romantic
advocates of authenticity defend this politics for overcoming the loneliness,
division, artificiality, and the subsequent social and political injustice that
men and women experienced in private life in the modern world. Getting
in touch with oneself leads to commiseration with others in a deeper, more
present way and, ultimately, to a more inclusive, just public sphere.

There is another politics that sees all this as conceptually and politically
troubling. This is the politics of theatricality (or, as I'll sometimes call it,
the politics of performativity). The most prominent theorist from this line
of thought is Hannah Arendt. While these thinkers differ on their ideas
about the public realm, they reject the idea of the centered interiority of
the self as a stable source of political legitimacy, seeing the Rousseauist
subject as fiction. Existentially, the inner self for these thinkers is a mysterious realm that is never at rest nor unified, as it must be for Rousseau's

© The Author(s) 2019
D. J. McCool, *Three Frames of Modern Politics*,
https://doi.org/10.1007/978-3-319-95648-0_3

political vision to exist. Further, the self is too evasive to be judged by, or projected into, the public without being sharpened by public masks. In this chapter, we will explore this alternative vision of the self in politics and its influence in order to better understand the discourse on authenticity.

The most systematic thinker of performative politics in the twentieth century is Hannah Arendt. Arendt was a German-born Jew who escaped the Holocaust and later became controversial for her statements about the cause of it, some arguing that she gave a moral excuse to Eichmann and other Nazi officials. She sees the problems of mass society and twentieth-century totalitarianism arising largely out of Rousseauist authenticity, its offshoots of intimacy and transparency among and between modern citizens, the authoritarian methods to achieve it, and an organic view of history that dangerously views these outcomes as inevitable. Like Rousseau, she laments the loss of self in modernity, but the subjects of self and politics are quite different for her. She rejects the type of Rousseauist subjectivity that attempts to unify the self psychologically, apart from the community, and then to maintain that autonomy in one's political experiences. Instead, she seeks to create a politics in which the public sphere is a space in which one can individuate oneself from others.

PHILOSOPHY AND POLITICS

The most pervasive problem in the modern world, for Arendt, is the dislike of politics. We can see this in our own contemporary political culture, as politics, and politicians, are routinely derided but "outsiders" seeking to "shake up the system" or "drain the swamp." To find the root of our antipolitical ethos, Arendt calls into question many assumptions of the Western metaphysical tradition from Plato onward. The integrity of politics was downgraded for Plato, Arendt argues, after the trial of Socrates in which his persuasion, "the highest, truly political art," failed to convince the Athenian jury of his metaphysical truth. In response to the trial, Plato's anti-Socratic, and "furious denunciation of *doxa* … became one of the cornerstones of his concept of truth." Rejecting *doxa* ("opinion") as a lower form of knowledge, Plato "yearn[ed] for absolute standards" which he then sought to introduce "into the realm of human affairs where, without such transcending standards, everything remains relative." Not surprisingly, Plato's later dialogue *Phaedo* sought to compel his audience through myths about rewards and punishments in the afterlife rather than through the use of persuasive reason.[1] Plato's "tyranny of truth" then attempted to take philosophy, which involved absolute, and impose it on the relative, fluctuating, and temporal world of politics.[2]

An analogous conflict that Arendt highlighted in Plato was between "two diametrically opposed ways of life—the life of the philosopher … and the way of life of the citizen."[3] Harkening back to the allegory of the cave, the philosopher contemplates truth in solitude. The realm that the philosopher contemplates is the otherworldly realm of the forms. The real world, in which citizens live together, is merely representation of that otherworldly realm. Like Plato, Rousseau and his revolutionary brethren sought to collapse these categories of otherworldly and worldly, truth and politics, philosopher and citizen. And similarly, Rousseau imagined his ideal truth-teller as someone who reached self-realization in solitude, away from the bustling bourgeois political sphere. Unlike for Plato and ancient and medieval metaphysicians, Rousseau's modern depository of this truth was not a well-ordered cosmos but the individual human soul. Yet, for each, public speech was to be direct, and the content of one's speech was to be truthful rather than theatrical. Telling the truth was, for Plato, a way to elevate oneself above mere mortals. Plato's specific purpose of truth-telling, argues Mathew Sharpe, is much more spiritual and otherworldly than it is political and worldly. Sharpe details how truth-telling, in Michel Foucault's reading of Plato, is not meant to persuade the many, but to elevate the soul of the addressee which, for Plato, ought to be "the prince or tyrant who, by learning to care for himself *only then* becomes capable of caring for others."[4]

We see here the tension between truth and politics: truth can be found through silent reflection and introspection of otherworldly ideas in solitude, yet putting a true idea into words before others instantly transforms it into mere opinion. As Arendt explains, philosophy always loses its truth upon its mixture with politics:

> As soon as the philosopher submitted his truth, the reflection of the eternal, to the *polis*, it became immediately an opinion among opinions. It lost its distinguishing quality, for there is no visible hallmark that marks off truth from opinion. It is as though the moment the eternal is brought into the midst of men it becomes temporal, so that the very discussion of it with others already threatens the existence of the realm in which the lovers of wisdom move.[5]

Arendt is asserting an age-old conundrum: truth and politics do not exist in an organic relationship; one must be imposed on the other. When politics is prioritized, the purity of truth often becomes devalued, mocked, and often punished in the world of opinion (as Socrates experienced). If philosophy is prioritized, it is often imposed by an authoritarian "tyranny of truth," as Arendt argued we see from Plato to Rousseau.[6] When philosophy prevails over politics, tyrannical regimes and subjective authenticity often become two sides of the same coin.

Privileging philosophy over truth has important implications for the role of the self in politics. For Arendt, there is a way in which philosophy's victory over politics tends to come from one's projection of one's inner self onto the world; one remakes the world in his or her own image. The possessor of truth has a personal will to be alone, outside the plural world of politics, movement and action among others. If the conditions are ripe, tyranny becomes the result of these personal, yet metaphysical impulses. As Arendt argues:

> Philosophers cannot be trusted with politics or political philosophy. Not only do they have one supreme interest which they seldom divulge—to be left alone, to have their solitude guaranteed and freed from all possible disturbances, such as the disturbance of the fulfillment of one's duty as a citizen—but this interest has naturally led them to sympathize with tyrannies where action is not expected of citizens.[7]

This is a common, everyday experience for most modern people: they want the outside world to come to a stop so that things are less confusing and they can retain a feeling of solitude, stillness, rest; a respite from politics. Yet we mostly accept the reality that we do need to live, work, and negotiate our lives among others. In the political realm, a tyrant rejects this reality, and if they can manage to suppress dissent, they impose their will on a world that is no longer a moving target.

Arendt's distaste for this kind of dangerous, absolutist philosophy puts her in company with anti-essentialist postmodern thinkers inspired by Nietzsche. In different ways, they see the demand for truth as a burden to politics, whether autocratic, democratic, or otherwise. Indeed, Nietzsche's own reflection on the philosophical mind led him to remark on the danger in linking personal visions of morality and the political realm:

> Little by little I came to understand what every great philosophy to date has been: the personal confession of its author, a kind of unintended and unwitting

memoir; and similarly, that the moral (or immoral) aims in every philosophy constituted the actual seed from which the whole plant invariably grew. Whenever explaining how a philosopher's most far-fetched metaphysical propositions have come about, in fact, one always does well to ask first: 'What morality is it (is *he*) aiming at? ... every instinct is tyrannical; and as *such* seeks to philosophize.[8]

Through different means, both Arendt and Nietzsche react to this personal-political mixture by endorsing a hyper-politicized agon. This agonistic politics promotes political freedom by avoiding "truth regimes" and the personal resentments of the philosophers from which they spring.

For Arendt, being-in-the-world (rather than outside of it) is a way to recapture politics. It involves thinking in solitude and masked public action that rejects the absolute metaphysical adherence to truth that Plato, and later Rousseau, injected into politics. Before outlining these, it is necessary to detail those modern anti-political, anti-democratic developments to which Arendt is responding: the rise of "the social" and the emergence of totalitarianism.

THE RISE OF THE SOCIAL

The social, for Arendt, is a new category in modernity. In this new realm of "society," what had always been considered to be outside of the public sphere, whether hidden away in the private household or the human heart, became subject to governmental administration and public judgment. Arendt details the injection of household items into the public realm:

[W]ith the rise of society, that is, the rise of the "household" (*oikia*) or of economic activities to the public realm, housekeeping and all matters pertaining formerly to the private sphere of the family have become a "collective" concern.[9]

Economics became increasingly handled by a "nation-wide administration of housekeeping,"[10] governed by "bureaucracy, the rule of nobody."[11] The rise of the social gave us the complete opposite of the ideal of heroic individuation Arendt admires from ancient Greek citizenship. In the Greek world

the public realm itself, the *polis*, was permeated by a fiercely atonal spirit, where everybody had constantly to distinguish himself from all others, to show through unique deeds or achievements that he was the best of all. The public realm, in other words, was reserved for individuality; it was the place where men could show who they really and inexchangably were.[12]

The rise of the social, by contrast, created an "automatism in human affairs" eradicating the space for individuation[13] or, as Arendt also refers to it, "disclosure" of the self.[14] As the public sphere was lost in the modern world, so too was the potential for the crucial *movement* from private to public that was the hallmark of excellence in Greek society. There existed no space between private and public over which the heroic individual could leap into action to perform excellent deeds. Everyone existed in public all the time, expected to exhibit their private selves. With the rise of the social, we saw "the disappearance of the gulf that the ancients had to cross daily to transcend the narrow realm of the household and 'rise' into the realm of politics."[15] Hence for Arendt, the loss of the public sphere went hand in hand with the loss of a heroic individuality in which one could individuate oneself from others.

Yet even more boundless and murky than the politicization of housekeeping was the politicization of Rousseau's *sentiment interieur*, a completely new conceptual realm of individual psychology in modernity:

> The first articulate explorer and to an extent even theorist of intimacy was Jean-Jacques Rousseau ... He arrived at his discovery through a rebellion not against the oppression of the state but against society's unbearable perversion of the human heart, its intrusion upon an innermost region in which man until then had needed no special protection. The intimacy of the human heart, unlike the private household, has no objective tangible place in the world, nor can the society against which it protests and asserts itself be localized with the same certainty as the public space. To Rousseau, both the intimate and the social were, rather, subjective modes of human existence ... The modern individual and his endless conflicts, his inability either to be at home in society or to live outside it altogether, his ever-changing moods and the radical subjectivism of his emotional life, was born in this rebellion of the heart.[16]

As Arendt reads it, alienation meant that the *sentiment interieur* lacked any solid grounding in either personal or public existence. His radical subjectivism attempted to locate it by collapsing these spaces. But in doing this, he further alienated individuals by robbing them both of an inner self and of a public self. Rousseau's radical individuality merged with radical communitarianism in a way that made either possibility meaningless: to be alone, in isolation, guided only by one's own natural instincts, was as lonely, thoughtless, and groundless as repeating totalitarian slogans among the mass.

THE FRENCH REVOLUTION

For Arendt, the French Revolution was the first moment in which the rise of the social and its constituent parts of authenticity, intimacy, and compassion was on full display. As a modern, fiercely secular phenomenon, the Revolution placed the depository of truth within the heart individual rather than in the cosmos or the heavens. As she tells it, political delegitimization under this new politics was earned not through ignorance of the external cosmic order, as it had been for Plato, but willful hypocrisy from within. The collectivist, revolutionary project of the Jacobins was to create transparency between the inner motives of the individual will and what the public saw and judged, so that the cardinal sin of hypocrisy could be checked and disciplined. In doing this, the Revolution had to freeze the fluctuation and plurality of politics and the inner plurality that was conditioned by it. They thus demanded that the individual's will to tell the truth become the *sine qua non* of politics. The Rousseauist universalization of "man" then collectivized this demand on the individual. As Arendt notes, "the very attraction of Rousseau's theory for the men of the French Revolution was that he apparently had found a highly ingenious means to put a multitude into the place of a single person; for the general will was nothing more or less than what bound the many into one."[17] According to Dana Villa, Arendt shows how after reducing the collectivity to one, the revolutionary project of making a transparent society could begin: "manifest in Rousseau's theory and Robespierre's practice was a cult of the 'natural' man, of the authentic or roleless individual, coupled with a ruthless politics of unmasking."[18]

For Rousseau, the public presentation of authentic, inborn compassion of this roleless individual is supposed to lessen one's reliance on others, avoid self-alienation, and thus maintain one's individual freedom. However, the politics that results from Rousseau's theory, argues Arendt, becomes not a public celebration of the unique authenticity of each individual but the forced requirement that each must act *as if* one is acting sincerely from within. Once the "war upon hypocrisy" is put into revolutionary practice by Robespierre, "public words and deeds are seen as either self-serving (and therefore false) or the expression of the actor's 'true' authentic self."[19] Only the appearance of the latter guarantees one a legitimate place in the polity while the former invites paranoia and violence toward the individual. Lionel Trilling notes that for Arendt, French revolutionaries grew paranoid over the "hypocrisy of the individual" and "the troubled ambiguity of the personal life, the darkness of man's unknowable heart." This paranoia forces individuals to conform to a widespread fealty to revolutionary ideals regardless of dictates of their inner selves, since "what was private and unknown might be presumed to be subversive of the public good."[20]

COMPASSION

A further element of the politics of authenticity that accompanied the rise of the social was the natural human trait of compassion. Compassion became equated with citizen virtue and it served many purposes. Firstly, for Rousseau specifically, it served as an existential antidote to the condition of loneliness in modernity. The maelstrom of urban bourgeois life that Rousseau experienced, in which he saw modern men and women perform roles for each other in a public competition, led him to remark "I am never more lonely than when I'm in the crowd."[21] He could not see behind the costumes and into the beings of the bustling city-dwellers around him, and he conjectured that their pretended manners were mere playacting while they secretly plotted against their opponents. Compassion, as the antidote to egoism, would also thus be the antidote to the loneliness that egoism engendered. The second, related purpose of compassion in Rousseauist political life was that it served as a social glue that allowed individuals to remain authentic, while commiserating with others in a tightly knit community. Because compassion is a latent, natural trait for human beings, practicing it would return us to our natural, authentic selves. Lastly, compassion was valuable in the French Revolution's reaction against the poverty that resulted from such a competitive society. The "heartlessness of reason" that characterized salon life and the "glaring indifference towards the suffering [of others]" among elites led Rousseau and later Robespierre to elevate the poor to high moral ground.[22]

For Arendt, the politicizing of compassion is devious. It is the fuel that fires the paranoid desire to unmask public actors and steer them in the direction of utopian political projects. George Kateb notes:

Arendt finds in the sense of suffering, in compassion and pity, the trigger for further extremisms of response, including the implacable urge to unmask the hypocrisy (real or imputed or imagined) of all those whose position in life automatically makes them suspect. They may be hiding something, some hostility to the Revolution, some resistance to the needs of the people, some incapacity to really feel the sufferings of others as though their own, some silent treason of the heart.[23]

Arendt argues that the role of compassion in the French Revolution was destructive of political freedom for two further reasons. Firstly, by praising the suffering of the poor, argues Arendt, it served as a pretext for Robespierre's "lust for power."[24] Here we can see that compassion and power do not mix well. As Margaret Canovan notes, Arendt does not deny the goodness of compassion; she only insists that it can turn into a "disguise for power-seeking" once it is taken out of "the sphere of direct, face-to-face personal relationships and becomes entangled with politics."[25] Secondly, beyond Robespierre's ambition, compassion destroys the essential space between individuals that is necessary for the painstaking work of politics, careful communication, and compromise, and replaces it with mob rule and violence. Arendt notes:

[c]ompassion abolishes the distance, the worldly space between men where politics matters, the whole realm of human affairs, are located ... As a rule, it is not compassion which sets out to change worldly conditions in order to ease human suffering, but if it does, it will shun drawn-out wearisome processes of persuasion, negotiation, and compromise, which are the processes of law and politics, and lend its voice to the suffering itself, which must claim for swift, and direct action, that is, for action with the means of violence.[26]

Rousseau's *Emile* shows us how compassion would keep the self intact while acting as a communitarian adhesive that would overcome the atomization of the self. For Arendt, in a rather conservative way, rather than maintaining the self and community, compassion fuels rage and prevents rational deliberation, destroying both the self and the ability for different factions in the community to compromise. Certainly there are many examples showing the power of rage to destroy deliberative politics both throughout history and in contemporary politics. Compassion (and its common counterpart, rage) for those perceived as the downtrodden, occluded, mocked, or disenfranchised has always fueled populist revolts from Andrew Jackson, to the Civil Rights Movement, to Trumpism. We must, however, consider whether political agency, even to engage in procedural politics, is at all possible without the injection of non-tangibles like compassion and even rage, into the public sphere. This is a question to which we will return.

MASS CULTURE

For Arendt, the politics of authenticity clearly facilitated The Terror by collapsing the public and private spheres, creating the social, or what Hanna Pitkin calls "the blob."[27] This set the stage for the emergence of "the mass." Twentieth-century technological advances and population growth created the conditions under which this monster could thrive. The mass became both victim and embodiment of this creature. It was a new form of social organization in modernity characterized by large numbers of people who share little in common except widespread political indifference:

> Masses are not held together by a consciousness of common interest and they lack that specific class articulateness ... The term masses applies only where we deal with people who either because of sheer numbers, or indifference, or a combination of both, cannot be integrated into any organization based on common interest, into political parties or municipal governments or professional organizations or trade unions. Potentially they exist in every country and form the majority of those large numbers of neutral, politically indifferent people who never join a party and hardly ever go to the polls.[28]

The modern individual, who had already lost the public world through the earlier rise of the social, became the lonely (even while in a crowd), confused figure of "mass man." Mass man is characterized by

> his loneliness—and loneliness is neither isolation nor solitude—regardless of his adaptability; his excitability and lack of standards; his capacity for consumption, accompanied by inability to judge, or even to distinguish; above all, his egocentricity ....[29]

In every way, mass man fails to live up to the ideal citizen of the ancient Greek world. The Greek citizen created works of art that would individuate oneself in public and that would then last beyond one's life, solidifying one's immortality in the *polis*. By contrast, mass man *consumes* fleeting cultural objects. Mass society, says Arendt, "wants not culture but entertainment, and the wares offered by the entertainment industry are indeed consumed by society just like any other consumer goods."[30] Not long before this, Horkheimer and Adorno had similarly equated the lack of an individuating politics with the homogenizing power of mass cultural consumption:

> The relentless unity of the culture industry bears witness to the emergent unity of politics. Sharp distinctions like those between A and B films, or between short stories published in magazines in different price segments, do not so much reflect real differences as assist in the classification, organization, and identification of consumers. Something is provided for everyone so that no one can escape; differences are hammered home and propagated.[31]

This lack of escape from the all-encompassing power of capital to shape thoughts and behaviors was a common anxiety among Neo-Marxist theorists of the twentieth century. But unlike for Marx—and his revolutionary predecessor Rousseau—Arendt claimed that the malaise of mass man was conditioned not by a lack of class- or self-consciousness, nor primarily from the power of capital, but on the absence of worldliness. As she argues, our "alienation from the world" is something that "since Rousseau [has been] mistaken for self-alienation."[32] In other words, it was not, for Arendt, the absence of a unified *inner* self that led to the conditions of loneliness and groundlessness for the self (as it was for Rousseau, Marx, and authentic politics), but the lack of a stable *public* sphere.

TOTALITARIANISM

World-alienation was taken to its extreme in Nazi Germany and the Soviet Union. Under totalitarianism, individuals enter a complete unreality of otherworldly ideas, detached from experience. Their ability to entertain contradictory ideas (i.e. to "think," as Arendt calls it) about moral issues is greatly inhibited. For Arendt, the long-term rejection of politics in the West by metaphysicians from Plato to Rousseau, along with the modern psychology of mass man, created ripe conditions for this radical escape from politics and the emergence of tyrannies of truth. Totalitarianism signals the complete eradication of the public sphere of action and, by extension, the complete eradication of the private sphere of individual thought. It unifies and then subsumes the will of individuals into collectivist, national projects, the ends of which are seen as inevitable. Similar to the logic of the platonic forms, totalitarian ideology, as Dana Villa explains, gives a "total explanation" for the "inner logic" that is working behind "multifarious appearances" so that these ideologues are "emancipate[d] ... from experience."[33]

Totalitarianism starts at the level of individual psychology. Modern fluctuation and rapid movement in public create a vacuum of stable identities that Rousseauist romantics seek to fill. Yet for Arendt, without a public sphere, identity cannot be formed by individuating oneself among others in the agon. Thus totalitarian government for Arendt, as Thomas Dumm notes, "relies upon the extraordinary condition of stillness to control those who live under its rule."[34] Arendt characterizes totalitarian government as "the iron band of terror" which will impose this stillness by "destroy[ing] the one essential prerequisite of all freedom which is simply the capacity of motion which cannot exist without space."[35] The state bureaucracy fills this identity vacuum with its own authoritarian vision of citizenship. Norma Moruzzi discusses the apolitical, yet identity-granting nature of the totalitarian state according to Arendt:

> The organization of the masses into a totalitarian movement is not the same as their politicization; mass movements are not social movements. Mass support of totalitarianism does not involve the broadening of political self-representation. Rather, it organizes the masses into a movement in which membership and opposition are defined by category rather than action, and identity is essentialized rather than achieved.[36]

We see here that for Arendt, once politics becomes exclusively about identity, it is no longer politics.

Totalitarianism not only destroys the experience of living in open space in which one can move, but the experience of living in fluctuating time in which one can see and experience change. Without the experience of temporality, in which the world around us changes, new ideas cannot be born beyond the ones that the political regimes introduce as the unchangeable and ultimate goals of political society. This importance of spontaneity to political life can best be captured in Arendt's concept of natality:

> The miracle that saves the world, the realm of human affairs, from its normal, 'natural' ruin is ultimately the fact of natality, in which the faculty of action is ontologically rooted. It is, in other words, the birth of new men and the new beginning, the action they are capable of by virtue of being born.[37]

The logic of totalitarianism eviscerated possibilities for birth or rebirth of both political ideas and personal remaking. Stemming from Rousseauist revolutionary practice was the guarantee of the inevitable dialectic of history in which individual freedom would be reconciled with communitarian justice if citizens were educated properly. If the script of history had already been written and dictated by the totalitarian government which controlled individual and collective wills, then spontaneous action was impossible. The government then, for Arendt, "makes out of many the One who unfailingly will act as though he himself were part of the course of history or nature, a device that has been found not only to liberate historical and natural forces, but to accelerate them to a speed they never would reach if left to themselves."[38] With space, time, and identity frozen in place, the fluctuations of politics came to an end.

LONELINESS AND MADNESS

Life went on for totalitarianism's prisoners, but without freedom of movement and change that makes politics possible. Within this frozen, apolitical state, widespread existential loneliness anchors the individual. Arendt's definition and description of "loneliness" is not conventional. It is different from what has always been thought of as mere "isolation." Past tyrannies, Arendt argues, had isolated individuals from each other so that it was difficult for them to act in concert. Totalitarianism brought them together in a mass. For Arendt, the experience of loneliness is not a physical separation from other individuals, but a psychic, existential separation from what Arendt's concept of "world," in which citizens can fluctuate: sometimes agreeing and coalescing with others, sometimes disagreeing with and battling others through legal means, so that the outcomes of political action are always left uncertain.

Loneliness can be thought of as "groundlessness" or "disorientation" in which while there is transparency among individuals in the mass, there is no way to test, workshop, float ideas in a shared public space, since everyone thinks the same about laws and policies (or, at least, are barred from saying otherwise). Held deep in one's psyche, loneliness is the experience of "not belonging to the world at all." The public space that is necessary in order for individuals to achieve their identities is gone. To fill this void of existence, totalitarian government creates what Thomas Dumm calls the "One Man ... writ large, a leviathan of loneliness."[39]

Through their tacit consent, modern men and women trade in the atomism of modern solitude for this new and far more extreme atomism, as long as they have the mass to feel grounded.

What led to totalitarianism was this sense of loneliness whereby the individual descends into a kind of existential madness; a detachment from reality that Arendt describes with the phrase: "when I am by myself, I am deserted by my own self." Having latched on to ideologies not grounded in experience, one loses both the pre-political capacity to think for and by oneself and thus the political capacity to act among others: "totalitarian logic destroys man's capacity for experience and thought just as certainly as his capacity for action." Without the possibility of ideological fluctuation in a shared public space (i.e. plurality), one has no way of even confirming one's own existence as a temporal, spacial being. One's thoughts and senses have no way of being verified by the "common sense" of others that exist in a plural world. If everybody thinks exactly the same about the function of the state (the end of racial struggle for the Nazis and the end of class struggle for the Soviets), one's unique ideas, reached through inner dialogue, are never confirmed by others, leaving the individual "lonely." This is the extreme and ongoing dread of Cartesian doubt:

> Even the experience of the materially and sensually given world depends upon my being in contact with other men, upon our *common sense* which regulates and controls all other senses and without which each of us would be enclosed in his own particularity of sense data which in themselves are unreliable and treacherous. Only because we have common sense, that is only because not one man, but men in the plural inhabit the earth can we trust our immediate sensual experience.[40]

George Kateb emphasizes the existential importance of knowing that one is known by others:

> Life's burden can be better borne—indeed, one can become reconciled to one's existence—not if one knows who one is (no one can know himself), but if one is known by others as he knows them, and know not as cultivators of the inner life define knowing, but as the great poets and dramatists exemplify knowing, through creative or mimetic power. Each knows that he is known, and knows others. This is knowing in a special sense—knowing as recognition, not as propositional knowledge. For this knowing and being known to be possible, there must be a public realm in which men are expected to act, and do act, by word and deed.[41]

In loneliness we exist, for Arendt, not in the common world, but in our own worlds, even while surrounded by others. To view this through an Aristotelian lens, we cannot achieve our humanity, which is only realized when we are acting *politically* with others (with all the fluctuation in ideas and arguments within and between individuals that that entails). Without this sense, we are left lonely, without meaningful human contact.

For Arendt, politics is theatrical. We should only recognize masks of others, not their inner intentions, since the mystery that lies behind the mask is not something we could or should attempt to understand. This presents a challenge to us: that we embrace our groundless, mysterious world in our self-cultivation, a world that totalitarianism and mass society attempt to correct. As Kateb—an adherent to the Arendtian distrust of authenticity—notes, only when we can think of the world as a "strange place," in which we resist the desire to understand the mysterious and unknowable inner lives of others, can we achieve a healthy "moral indeterminacy." The "Rousseauist community," on the other hand, "discourages independence of spirit."[42] Under totalitarian rule, the world is not "a strange place," it is all too knowable, transparent, and un-strange. Everyone assumes to know what everyone else is thinking at all times.

THINKING IN SOLITUDE

In a world of indeterminacy, where both our own selves and others are not firmly grounded, we would be compelled to actively *think* in solitude, apart from the mass, while never letting go of the knowledge that we live, and are recognized, by others. Roger Berkowitz argues that for Arendt, "the bond between totalitarianism and loneliness is the phenomenon of thoughtlessness."[43] This bond is most controversial in *Eichmann in Jerusalem*. In a totalitarian world devoid of the fluctuation of politics, both bureaucrats and average men and women speak only of metaphysical, otherworldly, and spaceless, timeless "truths" that have been propagandized into easy cliches making up "officialese." Berkowitz notes that for Arendt, Adolf Eichmann's thoughtlessness was manifesting in an "impenetrable fortress of cliches ... he feared, above all, to live alone, without orders and directives, cut off from an organization or group that would give his life direction and meaning."[44] Eichmann, like millions of others, attached himself to a mass identity that was wrapped up in thoughtless Nazi ideologies that had no need for debate, compromise, indeterminacy, or compromise, but only absolutes. In Arendt's famous concept of "the banality of evil," she hopes to return us to a pre-modern conception of judgment, in which it ought not to be assumed that evil acts are performed from the inner will of the actor. Rather, they are the result of the inability to think independently apart from the mass.

Given that mass society and totalitarianism are apolitical conditions, how does Arendt argue we can recover politics? The answer involves her prescriptions for a personal escape from totalitarian mentality and affirmative reengagement of the costumed self with the world. In this formulation, we see three psychological correctives to the totalitarian personality: thinking instead of thoughtlessness, solitude instead of loneliness, and *doing* into a common world instead of *being* in one's own world.

Arendt's concept of "thinking" is something quite specific. To understand it, we must conceive the distance from one's fellow citizens from which thinking takes place. Like for those who have urged the contemplative life throughout the history of philosophy, Arendtian thinking, according to Berkowitz, "requires a separation from the world, a passion for truth, and a willingness to let go of the affairs of the world. In the name of and out of care for the world, thinking requires a distance from the world." Yet this separation does not mean going into isolation into the wilderness, or a cave, or the confines of a tutor's chamber, in the same way that Rousseau prescribes. Separation from others is much more subtle here. As Berkowitz notes, "[t]hinking is a difficult business" which requires one "[t]o stand apart from the public [without] stand[ing] alone."[45] This distance from the world is not an escape from it. Unlike for contemplative philosophers and prophets like Plato, Moses, and Jesus, who sought truth by leaving others (and their opinions) to be entirely alone both physically and psychologically, Arendtian thinking requires that thinkers represent others in their thoughts.

This representation of others, for Arendt, takes place in the state of what she calls "solitude." Loneliness, on the other hand, is the state we find ourselves when we feel a complete abandonment from others, as we do in mass society. She draws the distinction between the two by explaining that solitude is the condition of having a split self in which others are represented whereas loneliness is the condition of having a unitary self in which one feels deserted by the world completely:

> Loneliness is not solitude. Solitude requires being alone whereas loneliness shows itself most sharply in company with others ... The solitary man ... is alone and therefore can 'be together with himself' ... In solitude, in other

words, I am 'by myself,' together with my self, and therefore two-in-one, whereas in loneliness I am actually one, deserted by all others. All thinking, strictly speaking, is done in solitude and is a dialogue between me and myself; but this dialogue of the two-in-one does not lose contact with the world of my fellow-men because they are represented in the self with whom I lead the dialogue of thought. The problem of solitude is that this two-in-one needs the others in order to become one again: one unchangeable individual whose identity can never be mistaken for that of any other. For the confirmation of my identity I depend entirely upon other people.[46]

Rousseau's authentic self is always unified within. But for Arendt, this "two-in-one" is the proper conception of the self. It later informs Arendt's essay "Socrates" in which she expounds on the philosopher's conception of the dualistic nature of the inner self and its relationship to political speech acts in the public realm. Paraphrasing Socrates, she says that "living together with others begins with living together with oneself." This "beginning" in solitude is not a sheltering of the self from the plural world of others, as it was for Rousseau's Emile; instead, it maintains an attention to the audience of one's speech acts. For Arendt's Socrates, to be "with his other self" means to "interrupt the individual's sovereign and unitary self [by] internaliz[ing] the audience." By thinking, one is "reproducing the relationship between "agent and onlooker" within "the sameself person."[47]

In this way, Arendt's conception of thinking counters Rousseau's goal that the self becomes "truly one" after developing one's selfhood in complete isolation from others. Thinking is possible for Arendt in a way it cannot be for Rousseau, because, as she argues, the nature of the inner self is conditioned by the fluctuation and plurality of others, both in their physical proximity and in their mental representations in the mind of the thinker. Arendt's conception of the private self exists, as Margaret Canovan argues, in an "endless dialogue" with itself that ought not be subject to coercion or moral judgment from others, but always acknowledges their existence.[48] This inner plurality extends to the plurality of the world. Politics reflects a world of fluctuation in time and space, not stillness; as she argues, "men, not Man, live on the earth and inhabit the world."[49] Whereas the type of officialese Eichmann engaged in requires an ideology that escapes the fluctuations of time and space, thinking requires a plural realm of others that is firmly rooted in this world.

In thinking, Arendt seeks to maintain a division between the private and the public realm, but compels us to represent others in thought. In this conception, there is a buffer between individuals, or a Nietzschean "pathos of distance" that is maintained so that one has the space to think apart from the mass. But thinking alone cannot recover politics.[50] It is only one's preparation for a common world in which men and women can live among each other in public and distinguish themselves "as distinct and unique persons" through action.[51] To prevent the madness of self-abandonment in totalitarian loneliness, one needs not merely to represent others in thought, but to *act* among others. By immersing oneself in a vibrant public sphere, we learn from others, and we gain the "common sense" necessary to confirm one's very existence as a worldly being. If we did not have my thoughts and words confirmed or challenged or acknowledged by others, we would either develop our own private languages, or we would develop an officialese, like Eichmann did, that was completely useless, since speaking it would do nothing to differentiate oneself from the mass. Unlike Rousseau, Arendt recognizes this need for the self to eventually be confirmed by others to be real: "[t]he problem of solitude is that this two-in-one needs the others in order to become one again: one unchangeable individual whose identity can never be mistaken for that of any other." If individuals remain in solitude without "being seen and heard by others ... it is as though [they] did not exist."[52]

THE PERFORMATIVE SELF

This eventual joining of others is not a communitarian move by Arendt as it is for Rousseau. While engaged in public action, we maintain our privacy by showing other people a public costume instead of our inner selves. George Kateb notes that this does not mean that citizens do not communicate or appear to each other in Arendtian politics, only that they do so impersonally, from a certain distance, as performers playing roles, rather than truth-tellers exposing their natural moral sentiments of compassion and pity from within:

> The heart is a dark place, Arendt says more than once, and light cannot be thrown on it. What appears—the words and deeds of political actors—is necessarily impersonal, even though it is revelatory of something distinctive about each of the actors, just as a writer's style is no outpouring of his heart but is nevertheless indicative of something indicative about him.[53]

This "something distinctive" is revealed in a filtered form through the public mask that Rousseau and other modern romantics despised. For Arendt, it is the part of the self that should appear in public, and must always straddle the line between revealing the public self but shielding the private self. Between the two dimensions of private and public, the mask or *persona*—which the politics of authenticity had stripped away—serves as a buffer. Metaphorically, for Arendt, the mask or *persona* in the ancient world "had two functions: it had to hide, or rather to replace, the actor's own face and countenance, but in a way that would make it possible for the voice to sound through."[54] The mask thus endorses public action while protecting private thought.

The mask, "affixed to the actor's face by the exigencies of the play," also gave its wearer legal status as an equal citizen among others that the Reign of Terror stripped away in order to reveal the roleless individual.[55] The private self was protectively hidden behind the public mask, so that judgment of public acts would be diverted "away from what goes on inside the individual soul" and focus instead on "what happens outside and between individuals: institutions rather than will, actions rather than motives."[56] With the mask, internalized private thinking could be protected from external indoctrination while the externalized persona could perform acts among others. This mode of citizenship differs from the one advocated by Rousseau, who attempted to create an ideal self with no distinction between his or her private and public roles. Unlike the nonpolitical Rousseauist virtues of love, compassion, and pity, which are supposed to connect people in transparent (and dangerous) ways, Arendt's "action," argues Kateb, "not only connects people, it connects people in a way that also keeps them distinct, separate."[57]

There are two ways of categorizing Arendtian theatrical politics. One is in its *heroic* form. Here, the mask gives one the space and individuality to act heroically into public life. Following ancient Greek conceptions of citizenship, the mask serves as a springboard, allowing the individual to individuate oneself by leaping heroically from the private realm into the public realm. The public actor individuates and differentiates oneself among others through acts and deeds in a competitive agonistic public sphere. At other times in Arendt's writings, the mask serves not as a springboard for individuals to perform heroic acts, but for a more associational mode of performative public action. Rather than competing against one another in the agon, this model emphasizes a politics in which masked citizens act in concert with the shared, externalized common identities. The associational model assumes intersubjective communication of public actors as equals in their political (but not personal) identities. It envisions a politics in which individuals perform institutional roles and follow rules of decorum.

In both the heroic-agonistic and associational-democratic models, the inner self is hidden. While the two-in-one of thinking prepares the self to live and act with others, only the outward acts that spring from such an internal dialogue are considered "political." Because politics for Arendt is something that happens "between men and so quite outside of men" rather than within them, one's political acts need to appear to others in the world that one shares in common with others.[58] She says that all objects upon which public deliberation can take place must "be seen and heard by everybody" in this space of appearance.[59] This means that such hidden, non-visible, and thus non-common private motives for action, such as a Rousseauist notion of "conscience," ought not to be considered properly political.[60] What is common to both—and what differentiates each from Rousseauist authenticity—is the *impersonality* of action and thus of politics.

Political theorist Brent Steele presents a similar view that public life is a performance, rather than an expression of the inner self. He argues:

> The social reality of the performance suggests that it makes little sense to speak about intentionality as an inner-state or interiority if humans are constantly preparing for performances. The metaphor of the 'stage' means that we're never truly authentic, that we're always putting on a show—or at least internalize the presence of an audience into our own calculations and commitments. Further, actors can engage in multiple roles to multiple audiences ... the performance itself may determine these multiple roles, but so do the expectations of the audience.[61]

We can see how this exterior presentation to the world was an accepted and expected means of communication before mass society. In his essay "The Democratization of Mind in the American Revolution," Gordon Wood describes how Revolutionary Era rhetoric in American generally was

> designed by the speaker not as an expression of his personal emotions but as a calculated attempt to arouse the emotions of his listeners. Rhetoric was the art of relating what was said and how it was said to the needs and requirements of the audience. Since the speaker or the writer aimed above all to make a point and sway his public, rhetoric was necessarily less concerned with the discovery of truth than with the means of communicating a message.[62]

But this type of communication has since dwindled, according to Wood: "Rhetoric today no longer means what it meant for the eighteenth century. To us rhetoric suggests at best elocution, or at worst some sort of disingenuous pleading, hyperbolic bombast lacking the sincerity and authenticity of self-expression that we have come to value to highly."[63]

William James strikes a similar chord as far back as 1890 in his thoughts on the inner and outer multiplicity of the self. Like for Arendt, we are divided between private and public selves, and our address is formatted to different audiences in the dynamic public sphere:

> Properly speaking, a man has as many social selves as there are individuals who recognize him and carry an image of him in their mind ... he generally shows a different side of himself to each of these different groups ... from this results what practically is a division of the man into several selves; and this may be a discordant splitting, as where one is afraid to let one set of his acquaintances know him as he is elsewhere; or it may be a perfectly harmonious division of labor, as where one tender to his children is stern to the soldiers or prisoners under his command.[64]

In Arendt, Steele, and James, we see a focus on the internalization of the audience and then the capacity to performing many selves in different public contexts. Not only is the outer world plural, but contra Rousseau's ideal, so too is the interiority of the self. Of great importance for both Arendt and Steele is the space from which one prepares for performance. On sociologist Erving Goffman's thoughts on the "back regions" from which performance is planned, Steele writes:

> Goffman's [theory is about] radical exteriority in this sense—because even in these 'back regions' where we are separated from an audience, we are still preparing for the show, still practicing the moment we go back on stage, and still coordinating our activities with others to affect, shape, and influence how we *will appear* in our performance. Intentionality is never subjective, then. It is intersubjective with those whom the actor must coordinate, and strategically presented towards the interlocutor who receives the act's performance. All those caught up in the performance—the actors and the audience—recognize it as a "ceremony—as an expressive rejuvenation and reaffirmation of the moral values of the community."[65]

Not only do political performers understand that they are performing, but the audience does too. Several times during Donald Trump's 2016 presidential campaign, he and his audience seemed to relish in the thrill that they were all tearing off the masks of prepared speeches, teleprompters, prepared applause lines, and canned lines about American values.

Yet, these staged performances are central to freedom under theatrical politics. Goffman's "back regions" from which we are preparing for a performance for others is similar to the private space for thinking, apart from the mass, that Arendt conceived. Movement from this space onto the stage of public life, and then movement upon that stage is, for theorists of performativity, the essence of political freedom. Unlike for Rousseau, having the ability to adapt to different audiences is liberating rather than alienating. All the while behind the public mask, whether before or during an action, we are aware of the plurality, fluctuation, and change around us, and thus no longer subjected to the otherworldly dimensions of madness and loneliness.

POLITICAL IMPLICATIONS

Arendtian performativity chastens the tradition of prophetic truth-telling from Plato to Luther to Rousseau in which truth is discovered outside of the public space of appearance and then imposed on the world. Arendtian politics prescribes that public speakers no longer testify to the otherworldly truth they have discovered behind the corrupting fluctuations of politics, but that they engage in politics on the ground among the fluctuations. The self is depersonalized, action is based on external political principles and issues rather than inner feelings, and public judgment is aimed not at actors, but actions.

With Arendt's dismissal of "truth regimes" in mind, we must ask if it is possible for Arendtian political actors to act in ways that overcome alienation while creating paths toward justice in the modern world. Can we speak truth to power if we are speaking through masks? Or do we lose our selves and do we become ineffectual when it comes to changing the world for the better? In the last chapter, we explored movements for justice throughout the Jacksonian period and into the twentieth century. They are part of the legacy of the American Left and were based on the Rousseauist fusion of the personal and the political. Yet there are elements of the democratic Left that embrace an Arendtian theory of action. I wish to outline some of these elements, each of which allows us to consider different parts of Arendtian politics. In doing this, we should seek to achieve the dual goal of achieving a more just society while overcoming the sources of personal, existential malaise individuals face in modernity.

Bonnie Honig differentiates between what she calls "virtue theorists" like Immanuel Kant, John Rawls, and Michael Sandel (we might include Rousseau in this group as well) and "virtu theorists" like Nietzsche, Machiavelli, and Arendt. Honig's critique of virtue theorists is that in attempting to overcome the alienation and contestation inherent in politics, they end up closing politics:

> Virtue theorists of politics assume that the world and the self are not resistant to, but only enabled and completed by, their favored conceptions of order and subjectivity. This assumption undergirds their belief that modern disenchantment, alienation, pain, and cruelty would be diminished if only we adopted their principles of right, established just institutions whose fairness is ascertainable from a particular (rational) perspective, or yielded to the truth of membership in a wider community of meaning and value. In short, each of the virtue theorists ... believes, mistakenly, that his own theory soothes or resolves the dissonances other theories cause. Each yearns for closure and each looks to politics, rightly understood, to provide and maintain it.[66]

In trying to end political contestation, virtue theorists "remove politics from the reach of democratic contest." This creates an occluded class of people that Honig calls "remainders." They are "depoliticized ... dehumanized, criminalized, or ostracized by an (otherwise inclusive) political community."[67] Remainders, Arendt might argue, are the persecuted "hypocrites" of the Reign of Terror who did not adhere to the truth-telling standard of the revolutionary doctrinaires. We might also think of our daily political discourse, in which office-seekers vow to not "play politics," promising instead to "solve problems."

Virtu theorists on the other hand, according to Honig, provide an alternative agonism that resists this closing of politics: "agonistic conflict is celebrated and the identification or conflation of politics with administration is charged with closing down the agon or with duplicitously participating in its contests while pretending to rise above them." These virtu theorists value performative politics in which the self is decentered and actions are depersonalized. As Honig describes Arendtian politics, "unlike private realm behavior, political action does not derive its meaning from the intentions, motives, or goals of actors." Honig goes on to note that for

Arendt, "freedom is not a subject-centered condition. Arendt criticizes those who take freedom out of the contingent world of action, attach it to them subject, and internalize it by attributing it to the will."[68] While virtu theorists wish to "call attention to the remainders of the system, to the insistences, cruelties, deceits, and inconsistencies, or virtue as a system of values." Virtu theorists advance a positive politics by attempting to disrupt the normalizing and exclusionary practices with which virtue theorists replace politics:

> Virtuosic action relieves the oppressive repetitions of nature, enabling Arendt's actors to 'establish relations and create new realities' rather than merely repeat old ones. And it subverts the 'rise of the social,' the forces of normalization that discipline multiple selves into modes of subjectivity whose homogeneity disables the individuality Arendt celebrates. Arendtian virtu ... has a role to play in the transvaluation of values, one that might embolden citizens for the ruptures, the genuinely discomforting pleasures and uncertainties, of democratic political action.[69]

We see here a close relationship in Arendt's agonism between dividing the unity of the subject, depersonalizing political action, and overcoming de-universalizing the subject. We should also see how virtu politics opens possibilities for an Arendtian moment of creation in the present, when one can individuate oneself through acts. Arendt urges thinking in the present—in which we cast off both tradition (from the past) and the centrality of the will (toward the future)—and creating something new and unprecedented in the world. What is valuable here is the notion that politics always remains ongoing, never finished, and always open to new voices of creative public actors.

Following the virtu theorists further, we can locate politics in spaces that they themselves failed to imagine. If politics is to truly to remain open, and always open to change, we should find creative ways to conceive that the personal can be political; that moral truth-telling based on personal experiences of oppression ought to be told in public. We can consider such an openness by illustrating the ways in which theorists have employed or critiqued Arendtian politics to find nontraditional spaces for action, and creative ways to combine the personal with the political. In her readings of Arendt and Iris Marion Young, Jane Monica Drexler presents us with a dilemma that radicals from Plato onward have always had to consider: "[w]ithin established democratic processes, oppositional action—to be counted as proper, legitimate, political, reasonable, even sensible—one must adhere to rules of a game that is rigged in favor of the maintenance of the very process the action wishes to disrupt." When acting among others, often we must first adopt cultural norms and engage in mimicry if we hope to ever be able to individuate ourselves. We must earn the right to speak truth before we speak it.

How can oppressed people overcome the fact that they need to act within a system that oppresses them, in order to change it? Authentic truth-telling becomes difficult on many fronts, especially for those in society who do not wear its formal costumes or hold its formal offices. As was the problem of truth-telling with Plato, as soon as truth is uttered to others, it becomes one opinion among many and loses its authority. As Drexler notes about Young, even if cultural pluralism and tolerance of difference is valued on the surface, the dispossessed in society are often at a disadvantage for two further reasons: (1) exclusionary "norms of articulateness and dispassionateness" govern deliberation in the public sphere, and (2) an underlying "structural conflict of interest" cannot be assuaged simply by engaging in persuasive argument.[70] Thus, if the exclusionary society needs to change, those excluded who need it changed cannot speak to it, and, even when they can, it becomes one opinion among many. Given this dilemma, Arendt, according to Iris Young, offers us an important tool: oppositional performative contestation. Arendtian rhetoric, for Young, could include "street demonstrations," "rowdy, disorderly, and emotional speech and action," "emotionally charged language and symbols" that "publicly ridicule or mock exclusive or dismissive behavior of others." By "shift[ing] the focus of 'politics proper' away from a strict distinction between formal sites of deliberation," Young is claiming to make room for excluded voices from the deliberative arena.[71] We see this in contemporary movements for justice on the left, in disruptive protests from Occupy Wall Street and Black Lives Matter, as well as from reactionary movements on the right: Donald Trump, while "authentic," is also a performative symbol that angry citizens have launched at the "establishment" that they feel excludes them.

Arendt is instead attempting to say something deeper about the nature of democratic participation: that freedom and spontaneity exist in the performative act itself. As Drexler notes:

What Arendt's theories suggest is that it is not primarily that contestatory, performative acts enable inclusion or recognition—although they may in fact do so. What makes these acts crucial for deep democracy is that within their boundlessness, spontaneity, and resistibility lie the very possibilities of political freedom.[72]

This type of immediate action from the excluded, Drexler points out, is not done merely to influence political outcomes, but are acted toward unpredictable ends; "the sheer act of doing" actions sends them out into a "web of human relationships through which they are filtered, challenged, and encountered by different actions and reactions of other actors."[73] Like Machiavelli's *virtu*, Arendtian action lies in "the performance itself and not in an end product."[74] We see here a similarity to Villa's reading of Arendt: acts do not necessarily achieve political legitimacy or inclusion for the claimant as ends, nor are they morally judged based on the inner intentions of the claimant, but they stand on their own to be judged, undirected, and without attachment to their authors.

The risk becomes that author-less Arendtian action—with all of its professed spontaneity, boundlessness, lack of a predetermined direction—is merely an aesthetic exercise by which individuals might reconnect with the world, but cannot change it. There were many good feelings on the left over the election of Barack Obama, this line of thinking sometimes goes on the left, but his presidency did nothing to change the systemic racism and economic inequality that plagues the country. Politically, the question becomes whether our politics has become merely a contest of symbols between left and right, while we continue living among masks and performances that do not challenge the status quo. Academically, the question becomes whether Arendt sought merely to overcome existential loneliness by connecting individuals in the sphere of action, or whether she actually wished to repoliticize the public realm in ways that pragmatic collective goals can be achieved to make the world a better place. In Arendt's own words, after all, she held distaste for the civil rights and feminist movements of the 1960s.[75] We can say that in some ways, Arendt falls short of offering much theory for those who fight for social change or justice. The root of this shortcoming is in her banishing of authenticity or biography from politics, which have given a voice for many (especially the powerless) to break out of the formal structures that protect oppression.

From a social justice point of view, then, what is formally considered "political space" needs to be robust and able to relocate away from its formal setting of public deliberation. We ought to be able to renegotiate the division between the personal and the political depending on the context. This renegotiation often requires going beyond the confines of Arendtian political space, defined *a priori*, to those spaces that are generated *while* people act. Thomas Dumm remarks:

> The problem with [Arendt's] conceptualization of space ... is that in everyday human terms space is not neutral and unmarked, an open and infinite entity; it is shaped by people as they interact through, under, and outside of demarcated social fields of life.[76]

We ought not be confined by locating the political strictly in a public space. Seyla Benhabib makes this point in recounting Arendt's nostalgia for Greek politics:

> What disturbs the contemporary reader is perhaps less the high-minded and highly idealized picture of Greek political life which Arendt draws but more her neglect of the following constellation of issues. The agonistic political space of the *polis* was only possible because large groups of human beings like women, slaves, laborers, non-citizen residents, and all non-Greeks were excluded from it and made possible through their 'labor' for the daily necessities of like that 'leisure for politics' which the few enjoyed; by contrast, the rise of the social was accompanied by the emancipation of these groups from the 'shadowy interior of the household' and by their entry into public life.[77]

Arendtian politics faces the same problems as Rousseauist politics because it essentializes the space in which politics ought to take place. Rousseau locks us into a stale, claustrophobic ontology of the unified self. Yet Arendt does no better: at times, she closes those windows to the private realm that allow the public to see "how the other half lives," which can then lead to meaningful social reform and the alleviation of suffering. Spaces locating the political and the non-political ought always to be renegotiated based on changing contexts and issues.

For democratic, emancipatory movements to succeed in their aims, politics needs to remain open. Politics ought not be closed down by confining it to the interiority of the self, as the politics of authenticity and virtue theorists do. Nor ought it be shut down by confining it to a space of appearance alone, as performative politics and virtu theorists do. Democratic theorists must always strive to locate—and relocate—the political in ways that avoid both tendencies to overcome politics.

CONCLUSION

Arendtian political theory is enigmatic. It offers us many, often contradictory, ways of doing politics in the modern world. It seeks to depersonalize politics while bringing citizens together out of their loneliness. It seeks to create a public sphere in which men and women can achieve personal freedom while preventing private matters from entering it. And it offers us a return to the agonism of the Greek polis while embracing certain associational qualities of modernity. Arendtian politics values depersonalized political action, in which the private spaces of the modern *sentiment interieur* and the traditional household are left out of public deliberation and judgment. Here, we can find both anti-elitist and anti-democratic stances. It can be anti-elitist in its hostility toward philosophical truth-regimes (with philosophers from Plato to Rousseau as the main culprits). And it can be anti-democratic in its dismissal of the politicizing of private grievances by the oppressed or those who claim to represent them (with radicals and reformers from the Jacobins, the American social movements of the 1960s). Following in the *virtu* tradition of Machiavelli and Nietzsche, Arendt seeks to open politics to new ideas and spontaneous actions. But these actions are instigated by external costumes that serve as buffers between citizens, rather than from internal expressions that serve to unite them in their humanity.

The Arendtian requirement for costumed political action fails to appreciate many of the most important social movements of the nineteenth and twentieth centuries, which relied upon the power of autobiography, personal expression, and shining light into private spaces of oppression. Our exploration of the proper spaces for politics must consider this failure. Yet we must take care to avoid a politics that ceases to end any space democratic contestation by collapsing the distance between citizens. In other words, how can we overcome the problems that result from the extremes of both authentic and theatrical politics to find a middle ground? These are difficulties to which we will turn in the following chapter on Henry David Thoreau. He offers us a dynamic range of modes for public action, and he also helps us to be alone while having the capacity to act together to solve moral problems.

NOTES

1. Hannah Arendt, "Philosophy and Politics," *Social Research* 71, no. 3 (2004): 427.
2. Arendt, "Philosophy and Politics," 431.
3. Hannah Arendt, "Truth and Politics" in *The Portable Hannah Arendt* (New York: Penguin Books, 2000).
4. Matthew Sharpe, "A Question of Two Truths? Remarks on Parrhesia and the 'Political-Philosophical' Difference," *Parrhesia* 2 (2007): 90.
5. Hannah Arendt, "Socrates" in *The Promise of Politics*, ed. Jerome Kohn (New York: Schocken, 2007), 12.
6. Arendt, *"Philosophy and Politics,"* 431.
7. Hannah Arendt, "On the Nature of Totalitarianism" in *Essays in Understanding, 1930–1954: Formation, Exile, and Totalitarianism*, ed. Jerome Kohn (New York: Schocken, 2005), 360.
8. Friedrich Wilhelm Nietzsche, *Beyond Good and Evil: Prelude to a Philosophy of the Future*, trans. Marion Faber. (Oxford: Oxford UP, 1998), 8–9.
9. Hannah Arendt, *The Human Condition* (Chicago: University of Chicago, 1958), 33.
10. Arendt, *Human Condition*, 28.
11. Arendt, *Human Condition*, 45.
12. Arendt, *Human Condition*, 41.
13. Arendt, *Human Condition*, 43.
14. Arendt, *Human Condition*, 179.
15. Arendt, *Human Condition*, 33.
16. Arendt, *Human Condition*, 38–39.
17. Hannah Arendt, *On Revolution* (New York: Penguin, 2006), 67.
18. Dana Richard Villa, *Politics, Philosophy, Terror: Essays on the Thought of Hannah Arendt* (Princeton, NJ: Princeton UP, 1999), 138.
19. Arendt, *On Revolution*, 96.
20. Lionel Trilling, *Sincerity and Authenticity* (Cambridge, MA: Harvard UP, 1972), 69–70.
21. Marshall Berman, *The Politics of Authenticity: Radical Individualism and the Emergence of Modern Society* (London: Verso, 2009), 115.
22. Arendt, *On Revolution*, 88.
23. Kateb, George, *Hannah Arendt: Politics, Conscience, Evil* (Totowa, NJ: Rowman & Allanheld, 1984), 93–94.
24. Arendt, *On Revolution*, 79.
25. Margaret Canovan, *Hannah Arendt: A Reinterpretation of Her Political Thought* (Cambridge England: Cambridge UP, 1992), 170.

26. Arendt, *On Revolution*, 76–77.
27. see Hanna Fenichel Pitkin, *The Attack of the Blob: Hannah Arendt's Concept of the Social* (Chicago: U of Chicago, 1998).
28. Hannah Arendt, *The Origins of Totalitarianism* (New York: Harcourt, Brace & World, 1966), 311.
29. Hannah Arendt, *Between Past and Future: Eight Exercises in Political Thought* (London: Penguin Books, 1977), 199.
30. Arendt, *Between Past and Future*, 199.
31. Max Horkheimer and Theodore Adorno, *Dialectic of Enlightenment: Philosophical Fragments*, ed. Gunzelin Schmid Noerr, trans. Edmund Jephcott (Stanford, CA: Stanford UP, 2002), 97.
32. Arendt, *Between Past and Future*, 199.
33. Villa, *Politics, Philosophy, Terror*, 92.
34. Thomas L. Dumm, *Loneliness as a Way of Life*. (Cambridge, MA: Harvard University Press, 2008), 37.
35. Arendt, *Origins of Totalitarianism*, 466.
36. Norma Claire Moruzzi. *Speaking through the Mask: Hannah Arendt and the Politics of Social Identity* (Ithaca, NY: Cornell UP, 2000), 122.
37. Arendt, *Human Condition*, 247.
38. Arendt, *Origins of Totalitarianism*, 466.
39. Dumm, *Loneliness as a Way of Life*, 36.
40. Arendt, *Origins of Totalitarianism*, 475–76.
41. Kateb, *Hannah Arendt: Politics, Conscience, Evil*, 8.
42. Kateb, *Inner Ocean*, 54.
43. Roger Berkowitz, Jeffrey Katz and Thomas Keenan, *Thinking in Dark Times: Hannah Arendt on Ethics and Politics* (New York: Fordham UP, 2010), 237.
44. Berkowitz, *Thinking in Dark Times*, 237.
45. Berkowitz, *Thinking in Dark Times*, 244.
46. Arendt, *Origins of Totalitarianism*, 476.
47. Arendt, "Socrates," 21.
48. Canovan, *Hannah Arendt*, 170.
49. Arendt, *Human Condition*, 7.
50. While Nietzsche's "pathos of distance" tends to reject egalitarian democracy and romanticizes a society based on rank, Arendt more readily accepts democracy's leveling effects. What they share in their reverence for a "pathos of distance" is distance per se between citizens, not difference in rank.
51. Arendt, *Human Condition*, 27.
52. Arendt, *Human Condition*, 7.
53. Kateb, *Hannah Arendt*, 94.
54. Arendt, *On Revolution*, 97.

55. Canovan, *Hannah Arendt*, 3.
56. Arendt, *Human Condition*, 183.
57. Kateb, *Hannah Arendt*, 26.
58. Arendt, *Origins of Totalitarianism*, 476.
59. Arendt, *Human Condition*, 58.
60. Arendt, *On Revolution*, 97.
61. Brent J. Steele, *Alternative Accountabilities in Global Politics: The Scars of Violence* (London: Routledge, 2013), 79.
62. Gordon Wood, "The Democratization of Mind in the American Revolution," in *The Moral Foundations of the American Republic*, ed. Robert H. Horwitz (Charlottesville: University Press of Virginia, 1986), 118–19.
63. Wood, "Democratization," 117.
64. William James, *The Principles of Psychology* (Cambridge, MA: Harvard U, 1981), 294.
65. Steele, *Alternative Accountabilities in Global Politics*, 97.
66. Bonnie Honig, *Political Theory and the Displacement of Politics* (Ithaca: Cornell UP, 1993), 3.
67. Honig, *Political Theory*, 5.
68. Honig, *Political Theory*, 6.
69. Honig, *Political Theory*, 4.
70. Jane Monica Drexler, "Politics Improper: Iris Marion Young, Hannah Arendt, and the Power of Performativity." *Hypatia* 22:4 (2007), 4.
71. Drexler, "Politics Improper," 5–6.
72. Drexler, "Politics Improper," 6.
73. Drexler, "Politics Improper," 8.
74. Drexler, "Politics Improper," 9.
75. Hannah Arendt, "Reflections on Little Rock" in *The Portable Hannah Arendt* (New York: Penguin Books, 2000), 231–46.
76. Dumm, *Loneliness as a Way of Life*, 37.
77. Seyla Benhabib, *Situating the Self: Gender, Community, and Postmodernism in Contemporary Ethics* (New York: Routledge, 1992), 91.

CHAPTER 4

Henry David Thoreau's Conscientious Performance

In the previous chapters, we saw that the disagreement between authentic politics and theatrical politics is grounded on two main interrelated issues: the source of truth for an individual's speech act and the relationship between speaker and audience. For the Rousseauists who promote authentic politics, the source of truth for an individual's speech is internal; it is discovered through introspection in solitude apart from the community. Once joining with a community, that truth is then delivered to an audience directly, without masking or obscuring that speech and without regard to the audience reaction. The transparency between actors and audiences creates an intimate political community based not on deception but rather on the demonstrably true intentions of public speakers. Public judgment, then, is focused within the speaking and acting individual, beyond her public persona.

For the Arendtians who promote theatrical politics, the external world of others provides the content for the individual's speech act. This content is discovered through what Arendt calls "thinking," whereby the thinker "internalizes the audience" for one's future action, thereby never mentally removing oneself off from the community of fellow citizens. The "self" that individuals discover through thinking is not unitary as it is for the Rousseauists, because it is reached through an inner dialogue one has between inner multiple selves that have been cultivated by an external, plural world. This politics envisions an agonal public life in which individual speakers remain opaque to one another. Public judgment, then, is aimed

© The Author(s) 2019
D. J. McCool, *Three Frames of Modern Politics*,
https://doi.org/10.1007/978-3-319-95648-0_4

not at the inner intentions of public actors themselves but at the external-ized words and deeds they perform.

How can we try to think about achieving the balance between these two models, when it comes to communicative distance, psychological well-being of citizens, and efforts to make the world a more just place? I argue in this chapter that Henry David Thoreau (with his fellow Transcendentalists Ralph Waldo Emerson and Walt Whitman) gives us a politics that can resist the self-alienation that each of these politics can cause in their extreme forms. He does this by presenting an alternative vision for politics and for practices of self-cultivation. Thoreau began his career as an educator in Concord, Massachusetts, and left based on his unwillingness to administer corporal punishment to students. Later he became a writer and transcendentalist under the guidance of Ralph Waldo Emerson, who would later provide him with the plot of land on which he would live and write *Walden*. He serves as a valuable guide for reimagin-ing a type of politics that can establish the integrity of the authentic self without losing oneself in the mass, as Arendt claimed the politics of authenticity engendered. For Thoreau, private life is left unharmed and is thus free to live in a poetic relationship to reality. It is free to explore the depths and multitudes of the soul. At the same time that Thoreau protects this private sphere, he gives us a politics that allows for personal expression in public that does not lead to a stifling mass identity. In his writings, he gives us not only a deep exploration of the private self, but different modes of public citizenship to be dispatched in different contexts. By oscillating between different modes of political action—sometimes personal and expressive, sometimes public and performative—Thoreau demonstrates a dynamic range of citizenship styles that carefully protect the integrity of the private self while generating public action.[1]

Presenting Thoreau as a political actor is not without controversy. Political theorists have widely dismissed Thoreau. They claim that he is at best a significant literary figure and at worst an apolitical wallflower who contributes no action into the public realm. Most pointedly, Arendt claims that not only is Thoreau not a political actor, but that he never intended to be: "Thoreau did not pretend that a man's washing his hands of [wrong] would make the world better … Here, as elsewhere, conscience is unpo-litical."[2] This depiction of Thoreau as an apolitical figure is unwarranted. Firstly, it misses the fact that Thoreau's privatism often shows his dedica-tion to pluralism. The provocative (rather than authoritative) nature of Thoreau's political writings demonstrates his understanding that he is one voice among many. He does not speak of "man" as a universal subject, as philosophers from Plato to Rousseau do, nor does he espouse any form of coercion by the state to compel a notion of civic freedom. Thoreau insists at the beginning of *Walden* that he is not instructing others, but letting them read his thoughts from a distance. And he admits, "I am confined to this theme [of talking about himself] by the narrowness of my own experience."[3] While Thoreau speaks from his own conscience, it is never as a universal truth for all individuals, as is Rousseau's, according to Arendt.

THOREAU'S AUTHENTIC POLITICS

We can understand the psychological beneficial sides of the politics of authenticity by considering how Thoreau employs them. There are several ways in which Thoreau may be seen as a "Rousseauist" who urges authenticity and sincerity in public speech. At the personal level, both Rousseau and Thoreau are traditionally cast as romantics who laud the psychological and spiritual benefits of solitude and hold disdain for etiquette in polite society. Just as Rousseau saw Parisian social mores infused with veiled manipulation, so Thoreau railed against the social masks in his time and place. His signature scathing dislike of conventions is peppered throughout his writings: "We meet at meals three times a day, and give each other a new taste for that musty old cheese that we are. We have to agree on a certain set of rules, called etiquette and politeness, to make this frequent meeting tolerable."[4]

At the political level, both seem to see a natural connection between the shallowness of politeness and the inability for their own societies to confront deeper issues of injustice, inequality, alienation, and brutality that each engender. People "go along to get along" without looking below the surface of niceties to see the rotten core underneath. In his politics, Thoreau often speaks the Rousseauist language of authenticity and conscience to highlight the need to overcome this dangerous indifference. He does this by speaking the language of prophecy in his public address in order to recover his own moral conscience in the face of complacency over slavery. He then aims, with his prophetic voice, to aid others in recovering *their* own consciences. As a mode of political speech, prophesy is Rousseauist in character, because of the role of the prophet, the mode in which he or she addresses the prophetic message to the audience, and the content of the message itself. This truth that the prophet announces can be discovered by the prophet either through religious means (looking upward) or secular means (looking within), as Thoreau notes in "Civil Disobedience": "I see that appeal is possible, first and instantaneously, from them to the Maker of them, and secondly, from them to themselves."[5]

What makes this mode of address authentic or sincere in the Rousseauist sense is that it requires separating oneself from the community of others so that moral truth is discovered from a unitary source, and not sullied by multiple conflicting, and often manipulative, voices in the public realm. In some moments when Thoreau is engaging in prophetic truth-telling, we see an uneasiness with the type of pluralism, including differences of opinion and action mitigated by impersonal formal institutions, that authentic politics tends to reject. According to George Schulman the danger in prophesy is that it "bears a vexed relationship to democratic politics" because it "lacks an Aristotelian dimension, an explicit valuation of ongoing political life. After all, biblical prophets invoke God's authority to provoke contest about pervasive practices long deemed legitimate, not to defend a pluralism of valid truths and worthy goods."[6] This warning shares much in common with Arendt's distaste for Plato's "tyranny of truth," in which the philosopher claims to have a monopoly on truth *about* politics, while actually thinking outside the actual political realm.

The content of the prophetic message itself pertains to the relationship of the community to larger social and political injustices. In his essay "Thoreau, Prophesy, and Politics," Shulman says that as an office, prophesy mediates between a community and the realities it does not understand or control. The role of the prophet is to announce to the community its moral failings away from its own founding ideals. The prophet does this through the use of a jeremiad, which contains social criticism within it, orienting the community toward its origins. In Thoreau's expressed hostility to "what is called politics" in his day, he uses the jeremiad to uproot everyday political passivity of complacency over slavery and imperialism, even within the supposedly "free" states in the north.[7] There is, of course, a danger in assigning too much authority to the prophet for fear of the development of a violent and undemocratic state of exception, but Shulman's treatment of Thoreau's prophesy sees it placed in a long tradition of American prophets who use their offices for counter-hegemonic purposes. This has been typical of the American Left, which has historically employed this logic in fighting identity politics of the dominant classes while embracing the identity politics of marginalized groups; given that the liberal idea that all are enjoying freedom and equality under an impartial set of laws and institutions is fiction, we ought not pretend that one ought not be "impartial" political contestation. We will discuss later how this idea has become increasingly a staple of right-wing rhetoric in recent years.

THE FRACTURED SELF

Thoreau's hostile stance toward intimacy is indicative of the Arendtian side of his politics. Like Arendt, Thoreau's corrective for the loss of self is the dynamic thinking that takes place in solitude, which Arendt describes as being "alone with myself." Once this self is recovered through thinking, it is equipped with political agency. Then, even in public, the Arendtian self never quite joins with others, but maintains a psychic distance; one is able to perform for others rather than *being* with them, whether this is to outdo them, to cooperate with them, or, in the case of Thoreau, to hero-ically shock their consciences. By adopting this self at times, Thoreau moves away from his Rousseauist romanticism; his self-recovery rejects the reification of the self as a unitary and moral agent. Along with his fellow Transcendentalists Emerson and Whitman (who collectively make up what George Kateb calls "the Emersonians"), Thoreau, when he needs to, leaves the language of authenticity behind and instead celebrates his own fractured and multitudinous sense of self. Relatedly, he embraces demo-cratic pluralism in politics. This is a politics that relies on the fractured self we see in Arendt-inspired postmodern theorists like Foucault, George Kateb, and Thomas Dumm. It is in these moments that we can see the flexibility of Thoreau's politics since it encompasses more than its authen-tic, prophetic, Rousseauist assumptions alone.

Kateb lauds other similar modern thinkers that share Thoreau's employ-ment of the decentered self, and describes the ways in which it is the best agent for democracy. In his book *The Inner Ocean*, Kateb advances Foucault's view that "[t]he individual is a product of power." He employs Foucault's critiques of the Cartesian self and the public power that creates it. Like Foucault, he defends the notions of the decentered self and a destabilized public realm. Kateb quotes Foucault, "[w]hat is needed is to 'de-individualize' by means of multiplication and displacement, diverse combinations. The group must not be the organic bond united hierar-chized individuals, but a constant generator of de-individualization."[8] Kateb ventures that: "the sort of group [Foucault] wants is a passionate but temporary affinity group. Each person will belong to many groups, serially or concurrently."[9] Even though he is often viewed as an anti-institutionalist thinker, Foucault and those like him share the inner and outer pluralism of James Madison we will explore soon.

Kateb and the writers he celebrates support an anti-Cartesian, decentered form of the self. He says that in their own unique practices of individualism, "The Emersonians" (Emerson, Thoreau, and Whitman) share an affinity with Foucault on the goal of de-individualization. Kateb shows how they transcend the culturally implanted "expression of personality," which conceives of the individual as a unitary being, by teaching what it means to be an individual that is always in movement, always changing, and always *becoming*. The self-becoming, for Kateb, that these thinkers advance, involves three types of individuality that individuals must achieve, at different moments of their lives: positive, negative, and impersonal. Positive individuality involves making a project out of one's life by "living deliberately." This involves deviation from a conformist style of individuality which is commonly mistaken for real authenticity. One could easily see Thoreau's *Walden* as a text dedicated to positive individuality. Negative individuality is closely related, since it involves the practice of "no-saying" to unjust and inauthentic conventions and laws. This is seen most poignantly in Thoreau's more explicit political resistance.[10] As Thoreau states in "Civil Disobedience":

> Must the citizen ever for a moment, or in the least degree, resign his conscience to the legislator? Why has every man a conscience, then? I think that we should be men first, and subjects afterward. It is not desirable to cultivate a respect for the law, so much as for the right. The only obligation which I have a right to assume, is to do at any time what I think right.[11]

Here, Thoreau escapes becoming a thoughtless, immoral citizen by "no-saying," and exercising his right to leave the community.

While both of these modes of individualism are important in themselves, they lead to the mode which *aesthetically* connects individuals in a democracy: impersonal individuality. This is an "awareness [of] democratic ecstasy" in "self-abandonment," moving "away from egotism." Rather than the expressive self, which, as both Foucault and Kateb argue, is the product of discipline, the Emersonians stress the "cultivated inward self" which allows one to experience "an opening onto the reality of the world." We see this clearly stated by Emerson when he says that in this state of being "all mean egotism vanishes."[12] In this state, the individual achieves a sense of immortality. As Kateb says, to be in this state "is to know that no matter how long one lived one would never run out of sentences to say and write about the nature and course of life."[13] While totalitarian regimes have an end of history in mind, democracy's possibilities are endless, just as its combinations of people, affinity groups, events, and ideas. For this reason, language, with its infinite combinations of words, sounds, phrases, and ideas, is the metaphor for democracy. As poet Joan Richardson says in her reading of Emerson, he believes that "[t]he sentence is the unit of democracy."[14]

TURNING INWARD AS PREPARATION FOR A PLURAL WORLD

Kateb shows how the strange experience of losing one's attachment to the world and turning inward can have democratic possibilities. Turning inward rather than externalizing the self is an important pre-political stage for both the Rousseauist and Arendtian models of politics for different reasons. For Rousseau, it is to find the unitary self which will later be expressed to others. For Arendt, the inward turn is meant to discover the multiple selves one possesses that have been cultivated by one's experience in a world of plurality, so that one can later navigate that plural world better. Sometimes, Emerson and Thoreau are too apolitical: they both demonstrate the ecstatic experience of the inward turn without much indication that it serves any immediate democratic purpose at all. But Whitman, who as Emerson said "brought him to a boil" after simmering for so long, is most illuminating in his illustration of the multiplicity of selves one finds when turning inward, and the democratic possibilities that can spring from multiple inner selves. He echoes Arendt's connection between finding multiple voices internally in the self and experiencing multiple voices externally in the world. This is shown in Whitman's famous assertion that he "contain[s] multitudes." Kateb details how the "hallucinatory quality" of Whitman's "Song of Myself" shows "an assortment of genres," a "dreamlike mobility of identity," and "the feeling that our nature is strange." This is rejection of Cartesian self-knowledge, since the poem shows that "[k]nowing oneself is therefore knowing that there is no single, transparent entity to know."

In his breakdown of any single transparent entity, Kateb's Whitman is also defying a "religious conception of the soul" in favor of a more secular conception, thus preparing us for the pluralism of *this* world, rather than the other world after death. For Kateb, "the direct and indirect lessons of the poem are democratic lessons in connectedness." They recognize the infinite potentialities within one's self and others: "there is always more to know about oneself than one can say" and "[j]ust as I am more than others can take in, so they are more than I can take in." This realization about the self and others has the effect of "intensify[ing] the mutuality between strangers, which is intrinsic to the idea of rights-based individualism in a democracy." "Song of Myself" is not strictly autobiographical for Kateb. When Whitman writes "What I assume you shall assume," Kateb says, "It is not that we must obey him as we read him ... if we understand the poem, we will see that the poet and his readers are alike."[15] They are alike in the fact that both self and others can never be completely known and transparent. This "not knowing" is what makes democracy vibrant, unpredictable, and a space for constant self-becoming. Thoreau at times also displays a playfulness about his self-conception that prepares him for politics. We can see the democratic significance attached to the realization that one "contains multitudes" in Thoreau's experience of solitude at Walden Pond. Echoing Arendt's call for the thinker in solitude to be "together with himself," Thoreau says, "[w]ith thinking we may be beside ourselves in a sane sense." Thoreau says he experiences "a certain doubleness by which I can stand as remote from myself as from another ... I am conscious of the presence and criticism of a part of me that is not a part of me, but spectator."[16]

Totalitarianism trapped its prisoners in an existential state that emptied the self of critical thinking, leaving it static, empty, and one-dimensional. As a free-living individual, Thoreau provides us an entire catalogue of the political and non-political dimensions we are free to experience in life. He oscillates between the experience of having a unified inner self, as Rousseau endorsed for modern individuals, and having a fractured inner self, as Arendt endorsed. And sometimes, Thoreau engaged in a more Zen-like abandonment of the inner self; of all "mean egoism vanishing," as his friend Emerson would say, and "democratic self-abandonment" as Kateb ascribes to Whitman. Thoreau also oscillates between political inaction and action, and then between different *types* of action. In his eclecticism, Thoreau gives us a way to think about the different constitutions of our inner self, the different ways we can relate to others, and the various ways we can attach ourselves to the democratic polity. In a free political realm, we ought to be able to engage in these adjustments and oscillations. Kateb calls Thoreau's politics the "episodic citizenship," which is a major achievement of "democratic individuality," where we enter and leave politics when we choose, or when our inner conscience compels us to act. So sometimes this means resisting; Thoreau's politics of "no-saying" in "Civil Disobedience," argues Kateb, is "a strong dissolver of the mystique of authority, first in the public realm and, ineluctably, in all others well."[17] Sometimes episodic citizenship includes tuning out from politics for a while. Sometimes it means taking occasional and minor political actions (like voting). Further, a culture of democratic individuality is not simply about choosing the intensity and frequency of one's involvement; it must acknowledge the protection of everyone *else's* rights, even those of strangers.[18] To invade the rights of others would be to deny the rights to infinite self-discovery, expression, and change over time that others afford to me.

This constant self-fashioning is difficult work. It is not the product of licentiousness, or of living on whims alone. In fact, those modes of living lead to the kinds of existential malaise that Arendt lamented. Living this kind of free, vibrant life requires constant creativity, self-engagement, and a coming-back to the world after abandoning it, whether physically or existentially. One must avoid stillness and wholeness for too long. By sensing multiplicity within his own thinking, Thoreau avoids the type of radical unity of the self that Arendt warns leads from a lack of thinking to loneliness and finally to widespread madness and depoliticization of the world. There are moments when Thoreau seems to anticipate Arendt's connection between these ideas. In his chapter "Solitude" from *Walden*, Thoreau describes loneliness as something that often exists when we are among others: "[w]e are for the most part more lonely when we go abroad among men then when we stay in our own chambers."[19] He can avoid loneliness by engaging in a type of free play that breaks up the unitary self Rousseau sought to establish. Through this play, he describes himself as

> a human entity; the scene, so to speak, of thoughts and affections ... sensible of a certain doubleness by which I can stand as remote from myself as from another ... I am conscious of the presence and criticism of a part of me, which, as it were, is not a part of me, but spectator.[20]

Thoreau avoids loneliness, which is the complete abandonment of everyone and everything, by getting outside himself, and finding company with the different parts of himself. He avoids going down a dark hole of loneliness, in which the wholeness of the self envelops him, and he cannot escape. At work here is the disengaged reason of the Lockean subject, who can observe oneself from the outside, along with Arendt and Whitman's self, who can understand and find solace in the fact that one contains multitudes, and is not, in fact, a one-dimensional being that is a product of outside forces, or existential loneliness.

Thoreau goes on in this chapter to detail an allegory that denotes the madness that can ensue in states of loneliness and the illusions that can follow. He tells the story of "a man lost in the woods and dying of famine and exhaustion ... whose loneliness was relieved by grotesque visions ... which he believed to be real." He links this experience to our illusions about "normal and natural society" which falsely makes us "come to know that we are never alone."[21] Thoreau's story of the madman relates to Arendt's vision of totalitarianism, in which lonely and mad individuals are lured into illusory visions of togetherness and organic unity despite our fundamental reality of separateness and opaqueness in the public realm. For both Arendt and Thoreau, overcoming loneliness involves recovery of the self, but not the authentic Rousseauist self embedded in a community. Rather, the pre-political self in solitude is a "scene" upon which one can playfully converse with oneself.

THOREAU ENCOUNTERING OTHERS

Just as Thoreau must avoid falling into a thoughtless, existential loneliness, he must avoid losing his self in the mass. His multiplicity in his own thinking allows Thoreau to acknowledge the fundamental reality of pluralism in the public world. It affords himself the mental space to engage in Arendt's Socratic practice of "internalizing the audience." For Arendt, this mental act allowed one to stay connected to the plural world of others, even when taking respite from it. Thoreau's internalization of the audience makes this connection with others as well, but also establishes the mental space for disconnection from this plural world. Jane Bennett argues that "Thoreau's project of self-fashioning" in solitude involves recognizing moments of what she calls "the They" within him, which is his realization in any given moment that he is passively and thoughtlessly conforming his thoughts and behaviors to those of others.[22] Thoreau's "They" is not only an external "audience" to internalize as it is in Arendt's Socratic mode of thinking, but a force to be constantly resisted in order for one to live independently. He must always beware of mimicry of others that becomes thoughtless.

Thoreau not only seeks to resist the colonizing of his self by others, but he internalizes the audience so that he can perform to it in public for a collective political purpose. Arendt saw Thoreau in "Civil Disobedience" as "unpolitical," since his action stemmed from his conscience (a Rousseauist impetuous for politics). In her formulation, it was not a self-initiated action meant to lead to any collective good, or primarily to persuade an audience, but rather a private act meant to publicly wash his own hands of participation in injustice. In order to satisfy an Arendtian qualification for political action, an act must be positive and stem from one's own political agency. Thoreau's 1859 speech "A Plea for Captain John Brown" meets this criteria. Thoreau's act of speaking in favor of John Brown, an Evangelical preacher who had slaughtered slave owners at Harpers Ferry, and was sentenced to be hanged, was a positive political act. Thoreau initiated this action himself (even going so far as to ring the meetinghouse bell to announce the lecture, which no one else would do, considering Concord's moral ambivalence to Brown's actions). It is at once authentic and performative, bridging the gap between the Rousseauist emphasis on public expression of the private moral conscience and the Arendtian emphasis on the heroic creation of an object for public judgment, one that is conjured by evoking a common principle rather than the character of the actor or speaker.

We spoke in the chapter on theatrical politics of the two different strains of theatricality: one moderate and institutional, the other radical, heroic, and often (like authentic politics) seeking to achieve political aims outside of formal institutions. Thoreau's John Brown speech is an example of the latter. According to Jack Turner, Thoreau demonstrates how

> the performance of conscience before an audience transforms the invocation of conscience from a personally political act into a publicly political one ... the aim of the performance is to provoke one's neighbors into a process of individual self-reform that will make them capable of properly vigilant democratic citizenship and conscientious political agitation.[23]

Thoreau used rhetoric about the Christ-like qualities of the widely despised John Brown: "Some eighteen hundred years ago Christ was crucified, this morning, perchance, Captain John Brown was hung. These are the two ends of a chain which is not without its links."[24] He also equated Brown with his own intellectual movements, calling him "a transcendentalist above all" and, even more shockingly, "the most American of us all."[25]

Thoreau ends by memorializing Brown's actions, with a rousing prediction that Americans will one day regret their persecution of him, and honor him as a major catalyst for the end of chattel slavery:

> I foresee the time when the painter will paint that scene, no longer going to Rome for a subject; the poet will sing it; the historian record it; and, with the Landing of the Pilgrims and the Declaration of Independence, it will be the ornament of some future national gallery, when at least the present form of Slavery shall be no more here. We shall then be at liberty to weep for Captain Brown. Then, and not till then, will we take our revenge.[26]

This rhetoric was shocking indeed for the townspeople of Concord. Thoreau sought to provoke from his audience an "aesthetic awe" that focuses their attention on the memorialization of Brown's words and deeds; the very types of objects Arendt sought to make the exclusive objects of politics, since they could be judged in the public realm of appearance rather than the hidden private realm behind the veil of the actor.

The speech was prophetic and authentic at the same time as it was performative. It was not "authentic" in the sense that Thoreau believed everything he was saying, but in that the source of his action was a privately held, deep moral conscience, rather than a legal or collective idea. The mixing of registers used by Thoreau speaks to the redemptive project in which he is engaged as an authentic prophet seeking to return the nation to its principles. Thoreau's statement about how Brown was "the most American of us all" was not only meant to shock, but to say something about the idealism of America while seeking to redeem its people toward a better ideal going forward. With this declaration, as Turner points out, Thoreau was lauding the idea of both Brown and America at the same time, even though the latter fell short of its ideals. Throughout the speech and elsewhere in Thoreau's writings, we see that Thoreau is not rejecting politics as a vehicle that can lead toward justice, but that he seeks to change politics from a meaningless practice to one in which individuals can exercise their consciences.[27]

THOREAU'S COMMUNICATIVE DISTANCE

A major distinguishing factor between the Rousseauist and Arendtian models of politics has to do with both physical and communicative distance between citizens. On this issue, we see Thoreau bridge the gap, both in his specific physical proximity to his neighbors, and in the way he conceives of writing. Politically, Thoreau's writing about societal ideals at a distance from his neighbors puts him in the tradition of the literary practice of prophesy. Many times throughout *Walden*, it is evident that the type of moral truths he discovers about his society can only be done in nature, at a certain distance from the artificiality of the city. In the chapter "The Bean Field" from *Walden*, he uses metaphor to gain insight into the injustice and ignorance he sees in his neighbors and in the larger political culture they create. While hoeing his beans, Thoreau stumbles upon archeological evidence of past native civilizations:

> As I drew a still fresher soil about the rows with my hoe, I disturbed the ashes of unchronicled nations who in primeval years lived under these heavens, and their small implements of war and hunting were brought to the light of this modern day.[28]

Finding native tools leads the reader to the insight that America was not founded upon a virgin continent, thereby calling into question widespread accepted assumptions underlying the type of American exceptionalism that blinds Americans to the systematic injustice in which they participate. But Thoreau is not in complete isolation and thus can hear the echoes of civilization from afar. During his archeological discovery, he hears martial music and celebratory cheering from afar as Massachusetts militiamen are deployed to fight in the war against Mexico:

> When there were several bands of musicians, it sounded as if all the village was a vast bellows, and all the buildings expanded and collapsed alternately with a din. But sometimes it was a really noble and inspiring strain that reached these woods, and the trumpet that sings of fame, and I felt as if I could split a Mexican with a good relish.[29]

As an echo, the celebration is close enough for him to hear it, and make a playful remark about how the sounds *would* have made him feel if he were among the masses in Concord. But, it is far away enough that he was mostly alone, and not emotionally caught up in what must have been a stirring, nationalistic celebration in town.[30] These are insights he would not have had in the shallow, bustling, noisy town square. Nor would have had them if he were completely isolated. Thoreau is attempting to strike a middle ground between complete isolation and complete social immersion.

As Leo Marx comments in *The Machine in the Garden*, that "romantic pastoralism of ... Thoreau ... is an embodiment of Lovejoy calls 'semi-primitivism'; it is located in a middle ground somewhere 'between,' yet in a transcendent relation to, the opposing forces of civilization and nature."[31]

We can read Thoreau's prophesy as a reformulation of one's political thinking from the position of solitude. This is the same type of critique and reformulation that Rousseau demonstrates in his relationship to the artificiality of bustling Paris which, in his mind, was also devoid of moral conscience among the citizenry, and thus any chance for justice. Yet for Thoreau, he avoids Rousseau's individualistic and communitarian extremes. The separation is not complete (as it was for Rousseau's Emile), and the end of his reformulation shuns the creation of organic community. Rousseau's contract promises the communitarian joy, intimacy, and togetherness of the citizens. But, as Jonathan McKenzie notes in his paper "How To Mind Your Own Business: Thoreau on Political Indifference," Thoreau's political contract stipulates that his membership in the citizenry always leaves room for retreat from togetherness.[32]

In his 1972 landmark exegesis of *Walden*, Stanley Cavell calls Henry David Thoreau a "visible saint." Cavell explains that Thoreau's distance of "one mile from any neighbor ... was just far enough to be seen clearly." This partial withdrawal into solitude and away from the community follows in traditions of Puritan Congregationalism, where gaining authority to speak involves a complex consideration of the source of truth from which the speaker is speaking and the opacity or transparency between speaker and audience. Cavell explains, "The audience for the writer's words and acts is the community at large, congregated. [Thoreau's] problem, initially and finally, is not to learn what to say to them; that could not be clearer. The problem is to establish his right to declare it."[33] Establishing this right involves striking a proper balance between acting as an aristocrat outside and above the community or acting as a fellow citizen speaking to and with it.

Thoreau demonstrates that he as political actor can alter what is considered private and what is considered public as he thinks and acts through time. The space of separateness that Thoreau voluntarily creates between himself and his community is not aristocratic (the type of complete seclusion from the populace envisioned for Plato's Philosopher Kings for instance). He remains close enough to town that his experiment in "living deliberately" at Walden Pond can both reach his neighbors and even occasionally be informed by them, but far enough away that his own ability to think clearly is not confused by the clamors of the populace. According to Cavell, the distance Thoreau has from his neighbors at Walden gives him the opportunity to "perform an experiment, a public demonstration of a truth … to become an example."[34] Nancy Rosenblum points out in her essay "Thoreau's Democratic Individualism" that Thoreau "does not allow detachment to fatally separate him from his neighbors. We know that Walden Pond was within range of Concord, and Thoreau remarks on how close the Maine forests are. Both are available to anyone, and neither is more than a partial and temporary retreat."[35]

In *Walden*, Thoreau's seclusion from his neighbors allows him space for living authentically. Based on Thoreau's location to his audience, Kateb says that Thoreau's example "is not an incitement to the life of intimacy or to a cult of 'personal relations'" but respects the "pathos of distance."[36] This distance is not too far, nor is it simply a negative protection of his selfhood; it also allows him to serve a positive good to the community as a fellow democratic citizen. And it gives us a way to transcend the strict private-public boundaries of both the Rousseauist and Arendtian models. Movements for justice and equality since Thoreau wrote have greatly benefited from their ability to negotiate and renegotiate these boundaries as they have acted. Social movement leaders in America have performed a certain amount of Arendt virtuosity in their political protests. At the same time, they have been driven by private conscience discovered in solitude, which sometimes breaks forth into the public realm at key moments, as it did for Thoreau with his John Brown speech one year before the American Civil War. As noted in the chapter on authentic politics, democratic movements for inclusion have found alternative spaces for speech and action that overcome Arendt's dichotomy, without descending into the totalitarian nexus of loneliness and mass identity, which resulted from Rousseau's extreme individuality and communitarianism.

RENEGOTIATING PUBLIC AND PRIVATE THROUGH READING AND WRITING

Thoreau's need for distance from his audience of readers differs from the communicative modes of both Rousseauist and Arendtian citizens. Public life for Rousseau should contain a high degree of transparency between individuals in his "festivals of democracy." Arendt's politics also promotes a shared public "space of appearance," but one in which the private self retains its opacity by remaining shielded from public judgment. In both cases, we see a politics where physical bodies and actions appear in public space among others. But communication and deliberation, in *Walden*, requires time and space between citizens that only a society of readers and writers can achieve. In yet another creative mode of political action, Thoreau shows how this can be done as well. As Brian Walker argues, this distance allows *Walden* to be a "cultivation text" containing a "take it or leave it" approach to Thoreau's example in living. It provokes rather than instructs, thus respecting the opacity and diversity of his individual readers and thus the plurality, while still being able to express a private truth.[37]

Thoreau's politics is more than simply just a mixture of authentic and theatrical models. He can be better understood by focusing on the role that language plays in his politics and the politics of other Transcendentalists. Through the very act of his audience reading *Walden*, Thoreau is always attempting to get us to find our own poetical relationship to nature that can overcome the shallowness we have learned from everyday social conventions. In this way, Thoreau is speaking to his audience not "authentically" as an expression of his own radically subjective thoughts, nor "performatively" as a speech act that is outside and between him and his readers, but through an alternative conception of space between reader and writer that goes beyond these two models: he is trying to get us to interpret the relationship between ourselves and the natural world parallel with him, through our own subjective experience of it. The writer/reader relationship replaces the speaker/audience one. Writer and reader are connected not through traditional conceptions of the space or time between them but through the poetical nature of language itself. Rather than this relationship leading to a sort of shared identity as the speaker/audience relationship does for Rousseau (a shared humanity cultivated from within) and Arendt (a shared citizenship cultivated from the outside), this relationship keeps both writer and reader connected through their shared subjective observation of the direct connection of language to the world.

This type of connection between writer and reader is only possible when we consider the way Thoreau and his fellow Transcendentalists understood the fundamentally poetical nature of language. Philip Gura points out in his book *American Transcendentalism* that the theology of the Transcendentalists saw Christian scripture (and other divinely inspired texts) not as prose but as a "primitive poetry of the soul" that was "draped most effectively in the imagery of nature" where "verbal signs originally stemmed from man's observation of the natural world."[38] Thomas Dumm says that the poetic style with which Thoreau writes about his observations of the natural world in *Walden* urges his readers to "work the mouth" and "read aloud the shape of the sounds of the letters that form the words" (employing the "gutteral g," for instance) so that the written words he is writing reconnect with the shapes and sounds his readers make with their mouths as they read. In this way for Dumm, "Thoreau hopes to remind us of the deepest connections of words to embodiment, and embodiment to the world."[39] Stanley Cavell's *The Senses of Walden* is his attempt to rewrite Walden in such a way that it emphasizes how its poetry gives us a direct experience of what Thoreau experiences sensually in nature. Cavell himself is trying to relive the sensual experience of *Walden* by sharing Thoreau's observation of language and thus share Thoreau's experience of the way his words connect immediately with the natural world. Even though we can share this experience universally, we need distance from each other in order to do so. In discussing visitors to Walden, Thoreau explains why this distance is necessary:

> One inconvenience I sometimes experienced in so small a house, the diffi-
> culty of getting to a sufficient distance from my guest when we began to
> utter the big thoughts in big words. You want room for your thoughts to
> get into sailing trim and run a course or two before they make their port.
> The bullet of your thought must have overcome its lateral and ricochet
> motion and fallen into its last and steady course before it reaches the ear of
> the hearer, else it may plough out again through the side of his head. Also,
> our sentences wanted room to unfold and form their columns in the inter-
> val. Individuals, like nations, must have suitable broad and national bound-
> aries, even a considerable neutral ground between them.[40]

Reverence for a society of readers and writers is something we see among all the Transcendentalists, Thoreau, Emerson, and Whitman. At the political level, this communication through the written word achieves a modest degree of communicative bonds among the citizenry, but not too much intimacy to suffocate individuality and suffer the pitfalls of mass society. Apart from politics, at the personal level, written language takes on a more spiritual dimension for the Transcendentalists. For Thoreau, Emerson, and Whitman, the complexities, ambiguities, and conflicts within the depth of the inner soul are to be sought in spaces shielded from public opinion and public practices and institutions. For Emerson, language is not primarily a mode of communication between individuals, but

serves a vital private good. It is a vehicle through which one can realize the change in oneself by changing one's utterances:

> A foolish consistency is the hobgoblin of little minds, adored by little statesmen and philosophers and divines. With consistency a great soul has nothing to do. He may as well concern himself with his shadow on the wall. Speak what you think now in hard words and to-morrow speak what to-morrow thinks in hard words again, though it contradict every thing you said to-day."[41]

Kateb states that for Emerson, language establishes a "poetical relation to reality" through the written word in which one can endlessly explore the depth of the soul privately. Kateb describes an "inwardness" or "depth of soul" as

> "unconscious motives; obscure motives, movements, and associations; the capacity to feign or be double; the capacity to talk to oneself; the capacity to draw things out by thinking them over; and above all the capacity to surprise oneself and others in one's speech and writing .... Language is one great source of depth, and its sole guarantor."[42]

Thus language, while vital for a limited and measured degree of social communication among citizens, is even more vital as a personal practice for the soul to realize its own immortality. When Thoreau says "I desire to speak somewhere without bonds" in his attempt to "lay the foundation of a true expression" he is saying something similar to Emerson's remark about immortality being the knowledge that one would never run out of sentences to write no matter how long one lived.[43] "Bonds" in this case refer to social conventions and pragmatic political concerns in which one must consider one's audience when speaking. As we have seen, this unrestricted freedom of speech does not always apply to public life for Thoreau as he must fashion his speech to his audience at moments. But in private, the ability for boundless speech allows for the constant regeneration of the self.

Thoreau demonstrates to his audience in *Walden* that in order to live in plurality among fellow citizens, one must first playfully cultivate the multitudinous self or else one will be vulnerable to a thoughtless and dangerous conformism once in public. Thoreau's cultivation in solitude wards off the extreme of existential loneliness described by Arendt by maintaining an internal dialogue between multiple inner selves. That cultivation of solitude is a preparation for the self to live in plurality as an episodic citizen equipped with moral conscience. The internal plurality within us both allows us to develop a conscience and prepares us to engage with the external plural world around us. The multiple selves Thoreau finds within allow him to act out these multiple selves in public. Sometimes the self he displays is without regard to his audience and is thus authentic and pro-phetic: sometimes it is crafted toward a particular audience and is thus performative. Thoreau not only oscillates between a private and public self, but is able to demonstrate different types of citizenship when in pub-lic. The act of writing for Thoreau and his fellow Transcendentalists Emerson and Whitman serves a communicative function but equally as important, as a private function of exploring the inner soul, so that new selves are constantly in formation to keep in step with the changing exter-nal world. Thoreauvian privatism should not be characterized as either a withdrawal from the duties of democratic citizenship or as an isolated act of navel-gazing. Rather, it is a great example of democratic individuality that finds alternative spaces for action to navigate the difficult division between private and public life, as we act.

Notes

1. Jack Turner, "Thoreau as a Political Thinker" in *A Political Companion to Henry David Thoreau*, ed. Jack Turner (Lexington: University of Kentucky, 2009), 2.
2. Turner, "Thoreau as a Political Thinker," 3.
3. Henry David Thoreau, *Walden, Or, Life in the Woods* (New York: Dover Publications, 1995), 1.
4. Thoreau, *Walden*, 430.
5. Henry David Thoreau, "Civil Disobedience" in *Civil Disobedience, and Other Essays* (New York: Dover Publications, 1993).
6. George Shulman, "Thoreau, Prophesy, and Politics" in *A Political Companion to Henry David Thoreau*, ed. Jack Turner (Lexington: University of Kentucky, 2009), 125.
7. Thoreau, "Civil Disobedience," 9.
8. George Kateb, *The Inner Ocean: Individualism and Democratic Culture* (Ithaca, NY: Cornell UP, 1992), 233.
9. Kateb, *Inner Ocean*, 236.
10. Kateb, *Inner Ocean*, 89–90.
11. Thoreau, "Civil Disobedience," 2.
12. Kateb, *Inner Ocean*, 236.
13. Kateb, *Inner Ocean*, 91.

14. Joan Richardson, *A Natural History of Pragmatism: the Fact of Feeling from Jonathan Edwards to Gertrude Stein* (Cambridge University Press, 2007), 77.
15. Kateb, *Inner Ocean*, 252–53.
16. Thoreau, *Walden*, 88.
17. Kateb, *Inner Ocean*, 85.
18. Kateb, *Inner Ocean*, 26.
19. Thoreau, *Walden*, 88.
20. Thoreau, *Walden*, 84.
21. Thoreau, *Walden*, 89.
22. Jane Bennett, "Thoreau's Techniques of Self" in *A Political Companion to Henry David Thoreau*, ed. Jack Turner (Lexington: University of Kentucky, 2009), 295.
23. Jack Turner, "Thoreau and John Brown" in *A Political Companion to Henry David Thoreau*, ed. Jack Turner (Lexington: University of Kentucky, 2009), 153.
24. Henry David Thoreau, "A Plea For Captain John Brown" in *Civil Disobedience, and Other Essays* (New York: Dover Publications, 1993), 48.
25. Thoreau, "Brown," 33.
26. Thoreau, "Brown," 48.
27. It is important to note here that Thoreau is not necessarily endorsing Brown's actions as political. In fact, John himself was rejecting politics. But by monumentalizing the shocking and controversial *example* of Brown, Thoreau himself is acting politically, in the Arendtian sense, by persuading his audience through shock value.
28. Thoreau, *Walden*, 103.
29. Thoreau, *Walden*, 104.
30. Thoreau, *Walden*, 104.
31. Leo Marx, *The Machine in the Garden: Technology and the Pastoral Ideal in America* (Oxford: Oxford University Press, 1967), 23.
32. Jonathan Mckenzie, "How To Mind Your Own Business: Thoreau on Political Indifference," *The New England Quarterly* 84, no. 3 (2011): 422–43.
33. Stanley Cavell, *The Senses of Walden* (Chicago: University of Chicago, 1992), 11.
34. Cavell, *The Senses of Walden*, 11.
35. Nancy Rosenblum, "Thoreau's Democratic Individualism" in *A Political Companion to Henry David Thoreau*, ed. Jack Turner (Lexington: University of Kentucky, 2009), 2.
36. Kateb, *Inner Ocean*, 97.
37. Brian Walker, "Thoreau on Democratic Cultivation," *Political Theory* 29, no. 2 (2001): 156.

38. Philip F. Gura, *American Transcendentalism: A History* (New York: Hill and Wang: 2007), 44.
39. Thomas L. Dumm, *Loneliness as a Way of Life* (Cambridge, MA: Harvard University Press, 2008), 93.
40. Thoreau, *Walden*, 91.
41. Ralph Waldo Emerson, "Self-Reliance" in *The Essential Writings of Ralph Waldo Emerson* (New York: Modern Library, 2000), 138.
42. Kateb, *Inner Ocean*, 236.
43. Thoreau, *Walden*, 213.

CHAPTER 5

Institutional Politics

Until now, we have been discussing two different models of politics that detail the relationship between the individual and his or her social world. In each of these models, we've seen different versions of the ontology of the self corresponding to different visions of community. In the politics of authenticity, the Rousseauist self is a sovereign being who seeks wholeness apart from others. Once fully realized, she or he enters an intimate community where speech is centered on personal expression. At the outset of the Enlightenment, Rousseauist revolutionaries based this community primarily on the bonds of national citizenship. Later adherents of the politics of authenticity have conceived of more local communities or, in more recent times, what came to be known as "identity" politics, in which one's class, gender, sexual orientation, or ethnic background came to define group solidarity, and individuals within the group expressed their personal experiences, often in emotional ways. In all of these cases, the personal is political.

The politics of theatricality rejects all this. Individuals, argues this model, are socially constructed, yet ought to maintain private lives that are distinct from their public lives. There are, to be sure, citizenship bonds among individuals, but only in their external, public personae or actions, rather than corresponding to their inner selves. In their public relations with one another, individuals perform externalized, costumed selves rather than expressing inner, authentic selves. It is vital for individuals in any free society, argues Arendt, to be able to leave public life to return to privacy,

© The Author(s) 2019
D. J. McCool, *Three Frames of Modern Politics*,
https://doi.org/10.1007/978-3-319-95648-0_5

in order to make re-entry into costumed public life that much more heroic. The personal and political are thus firmly separated.

There is also a disruptive version of the politics of theatricality that can be used for either radical or reactionary purposes. The radical strain is best described by feminist scholar Iris Young.[1] Here, theatricality in politics does stem from personal grievances, just as it does from the politics of authenticity. Yet, unlike authentic politics, speech acts are not unfiltered, unadorned personal expressions, but outward, externalized performances that often shock audiences with emotional appeals, in order to disrupt the decorum of normal politics. From a radical or feminist perspective, this mode of politics seeks an entry point for the dispossessed and downtrodden into the political arena, especially those for whom normal political persuasion is not an acquired skill. Yet, as we've seen with Trumpian politics, shocking, vulgar, theatrical speech acts can serve reactionary purposes as well. Donald Trump's entry into the presidential field in 2015 by calling Mexican immigrants "rapists" is the most striking example of the reactionary potential for theatrical speech.

We have also explored a politics that borrows from the best of theatricality and authenticity. Henry David Thoreau provides us a political model whereby we can speak our moral consciences without becoming stifled by the confines of an intimate community. His politics is robust, in that he provides different voices, registers, and tones for when he is in the woods and for when he is speaking in front of an audience. Ultimately, he demonstrates to his audience how to reconnect with our moral natures, without engaging in the type of authoritarian "tyranny of truth" for which Arendt disapproves of philosophers like Plato and Rousseau.

There is another mode of politics to which we turn in this chapter in order to place all of these techniques of the self into some political order. Institutional politics emphasizes the laws, rules, procedures, and organized structures through which political actors must achieve their political aims. The major benefit of this politics is that, in its ideal form, institutions with standard sets of procedures allow spaces for people to fight for their grievances while reaching compromises among diverse interests. The drawbacks of institutional politics are, firstly, its elitist nature: it often requires access to power, understanding of often complex political procedures that is often afforded only by political elites. Secondly, because institutional politics works slowly, real people facing real suffering can see the redress of their grievances delayed or denied by bureaucratic procedures and rules. When the polity is governed by institutions that bar emotion from entering their procedures, it can also be drained of its humanity.

Institutional politics shares more in common with the moderate strain of theatrical politics than it does with radical theatrical politics or with authentic politics. Institutional politics pertains to rules and procedures of institutions, while a moderate strain of theatrical politics pertains the *style* of political decorum required to better achieve one's goals *through* institutions. Senators and representatives, for example, need to perform as if they are theater actors; they need to wear certain clothes, speak a certain way, and, under certain circumstances (especially in the US House of Representatives), tailor their floor speeches to time constraints rather than just saying endlessly what's on their minds. Institutionally, the formal passage of a law, or the successful arguing of a court case, is more likely to be achieved when careful decorum is followed (although, in our dysfunctional Congress, the purpose of floor speeches is increasingly for the purpose of rousing attention than making calm, rational arguments). Thus, political action through institutions is often theatrical since it is filtered through institutional rules and procedures that require one to perform. It avoids the kind of raw, unfiltered, emotional, expressive political speech that the politics of authenticity demands, or the shock-value of radical or the more reactionary versions of theatrical politics.

Institutions must exist to avoid the extremes of either authentic politics or theatrical politics. When institutions are strong and robust, they allow for the airing and resolution of personal and group grievances that the politics of authenticity emphasizes, as well as the virtuosic political performance of theatrical politics. Without the guardrails of institutional politics, countless misdeeds and atrocities have been done in the name of "democratic" aims. It has become almost common knowledge that Hitler's rise to power, which aimed at restoring the "authentic" nature of the German *volk*, was facilitated by democratic elections that put his party in power. On the other hand, numerous social ills, inequalities, and politically alienating regimes have been allowed to thrive by a theatrical politics that is all performance, decorum, and pomp, without any real ability to solve social problems. The extravagance of Versailles before the French Revolution created an authentic backlash against the formalities and pomp of court life. Many American populists from the Tea Party, to Occupy Wall Street, to Donald Trump have argued in recent years that "playing nice" in politics only serves as a mark to cover our rotten, corrupt systems. Ideally, institutional politics allows the better parts of each model to thrive; it creates spaces for individuals to address issues that affect the lives of real people, yet affords the impersonal decorum necessary to avoid the atrocities of mob rule. Through well-designed rules and procedures, political change can happen incrementally; given proper representation, they allow time and space for all voices to be heard.

We will consider institutional politics in this chapter from different angles. Firstly, we will consider the basic theoretical considerations addressed by modern thinkers who sought to bolster institutions. Secondly, we will detail how institutional politics has been used as a counterrevolutionary discourse that seeks to avoid democratic mob rule (and the politics of authenticity from which is stems). Thirdly, anti-institutionalist critiques from feminist and left perspectives will be discussed. And lastly, we will consider the institutionalism of Abraham Lincoln, as he subtly attempted to transform institutions employing a communicative distance between himself and his readers reminiscent of Thoreau's. Noting the conservatism of this Lincolnian politics will allow us to discuss recent developments in American political culture in the next two chapters, both within conservatism and American political culture at large, that weaken the accepted legitimacy of America's government institutions. As we will see, this leaves the republic in a precarious position in which more radical forms of political action thwart the deliberative aims of institutional politics.

THE REASONS FOR INSTITUTIONS

The idea that politics ought to be governed by laws and institutions, rather than directly by citizens themselves, goes at least as far back as the ancient Greeks. Aristotle famously conceived of man as the "*polis* animal" who had to negotiate, perform, and work his way through the terrain of conflicting interests in a plural world. An important component of Aristotle's formulation was the ability of people to govern themselves through political institutions. While civil society was to be a place of freedom and movement (at least for the few considered citizens), Aristotle insisted upon the doctrine of "mixed regime," in which the extremes of democracy, oligarchy, and tyranny are avoided, and where "precautions should be taken against lawlessness."[2] Laws and institutions then worked downward to influence the character of the people: "Lawgivers make the citizens good by inculcating good habits in them, and this is the aim of every lawgiver;

if he does not succeed in doing that, his legislation is a failure. It is in this that a good constitution differs from a bad one."[3]

In both ancient Greece and Rome, frequent activity in public life was the *sin qua non* of politics. Many political theorists at the onset of modernity were rediscovering these ancient republican virtues. But the modern age assumed that individuals would be more self-interested, and less involved in community affairs. The founders of liberalism, John Locke and Thomas Hobbes, believed that the job of government was to protect atomized, largely apolitical individuals from exposure to misfortune. For Locke, this misfortune was having one's private property violated while for Hobbes, it was bodily death. The way they sought to do this was to legitimize impersonal political offices that stood apart from citizens. For Hobbes, depoliticization of the populace began the moment after consent. The job of an impersonal, Leviathanic government, far from being democratically composed of the people themselves, is to keep human beings, war-prone creatures that they are, in awe:

> The final cause, end, or design of men (who naturally love liberty, and dominion over others,) is the introduction of that restraint upon themselves, (in which we see them live in commonwealths,) is the foresight of their own preservation, and of a more contented life thereby; that is to say, of getting themselves out from that miserable condition of war, which is necessarily consequent (as hath been shown), to, the natal passions of men, when there is no visible power to keep them in awe, and tie them by fear of punishment when there is no physical power to keep them in awe, and tie them by fear of punishment ....[4]

Neither the natural, authentic, sovereign selves that Rousseau would later champion, nor the energetic, socially constructed, theatrical citizens of Arendt's Greek imagination were to be left free. Hobbes's counterrevolutionary ideas began the modern idea that alienation of citizens from the levers of government was necessary to keep the peace. Less extreme, but still alienating, was John Locke's focus on political institutions and laws as means to protect natural rights. In his *The Second Treatise of Civil Government*, Locke argued that the purpose of government was the "preservation of [citizens'] property," which was achieved through "established, settled, known law," and "a known and indifferent judge."[5] Laws are not meant to determine the inner, private lives of citizens (as they later would for the Jacobins), but are "limited to the public good of the society."[6] And unlike for the practitioners of authentic politics who sought to have their political grievances redressed in the streets, political power was to stay strictly within the bounds of a formal legislature: "[t]he legislative cannot transfer the power of making laws into any other hands."[7]

Impersonal institutions and laws affected republicans as well. Montesquieu is more sympathetic to the ancient virtues of a vibrant public sphere, yet gives *modern* republicanism a liberal twist, and thus its uniquely privatist ethos. While Montesquieu's sexual innuendos in his *Persian Letters* pleased certain licentious strains of Enlightenment thought, especially those who saw Rousseau's radical freedom as a challenge to prudishness, his later, more sober *Spirit of the Laws* published in 1748 examined how to carefully govern human interactions through artificial institutions. Like the counterrevolutionaries of the end of the eighteenth century onward, Montesquieu sought to guard private life from the concentration of power in either a monarch, an aristocracy, or a democratic mob.

Montesquieu's *Spirit of the Laws* is at once moderate and revolutionary. It is revolutionary in its modern break from medieval conceptions of the governing classes. Constitutional law scholar Bruce Ackerman calls this "the functionalist turn"; whereas medieval versions of separation of powers had conceived of power being divided between privileged *classes* like lords, commons, and crown, Montesquieu conceived of power as being divided between different governmental *functions*: legislative, executive, and judicial.[8] Conceivably, this made governmental offices accessible not to inherited power, but to those who could demonstrate their virtue, or expertise in properly executing the functions of government on behalf of the public good. These institutions, in other words, were *impersonal*. And therefore, so was the practice of politics.

While radical in its break from the past, *Spirit of the Laws* is moderate in its vision of the ends of government. The main feature that differentiates a despotic regime from a moderate one is not primarily the character of the office-holders, or even whether the laws are good (though good ones are better), but whether or not it is governed by impersonal institutions: despotic regimes were governed by the rule of law, while moderate ones were not. Furthermore, like his predecessors from Greece and Rome, Montesquieu maintained that separation of powers was needed to maintain freedom: "[w]hen the legislative and executive powers are united in the same person, or in the same body of magistracy, there can be no liberty … there is no liberty if the power of judging be not separated from the legislative and executive powers."[9] By keeping governmental institutions separate, this would prevent government or any one part of government from growing too powerful and interfering in social or economic life of private citizens.

The impersonality and objectivity that institutional politics claimed were challenged by the counter-Enlightenment. For Rousseau, theatricality and formal, impersonal forms of government institutions worked in tandem to create unjust political systems. Bourgeois liberalism, in its governmental form, had leveled out the alienating hierarchies of medieval society in which individuals were defined externally by rank, title, and tradition. But at the same time, this new political order created a new problem. It separated civil society from the state so the latter could allow for the dynamic interactions of freely acting individuals in the former. Governmental laws, therefore, were seen as impersonal, detached from, and constitutionally superior to the human minds that made them. The relationship between oneself and one's government was alienating. Liberal government was, as John Adams proclaimed, "government of laws and not of men." But as Berman details, for Rousseau, this is absurd, since "the state ... grew organically out of social life."[10] A government was made by humans and thus can be changed by humans. Since government is a direct reflection of civil society, it is responsible for its injustices and inequalities. It is not a protection of free, unchained actors in civil society, but a creator of chains directed from those with power in civil society; a "non-violent, psychic means for keeping men in their place."[11]

This merging of the state and civil society, and thus the replacement of institutions with the popular will, becomes an important focal point for modern reformers and revolutionaries. It allows for the possibility of government engaging in problems of civil society and reflecting them well, rather than leaving dynamism of civil society (which includes its inequalities and injustices if unregulated) alone to operate on its own. This critique of liberalism and the acknowledgment of the human design of government led to two vital elements of a Rousseauist model of direct democracy that would put popular control of government in the hands of the people rather than non-human institutions. Firstly, it becomes impossible to argue that social injustices and inequalities are detached from the concerns of government. Therefore, government can be used to correct for them, and in the extreme, government can address the underlying psychological foundations of social inequities (or, to put it derisively, it can "legislate morality"). Secondly, it becomes impossible for government by representation to be a true reflection of the will of the people. Government by representation (at least in the creation of the laws) creates distance and thus a lack of transparency between citizens and government. Because of this lack of democratic control, elites will have more access to the levers of power than non-elites. Government will always privilege one group over another, whether this is the rich over the poor, the established over the non-connected, or the representatives themselves over the people they represent. We see this in contemporary populist movements, which often argue on behalf of "the people over the powerful" by denigrating the institutions that entrench the latter.

While Rousseau railed against theatricality in Parisian life because of the psychological alienation citizens felt toward one another, he railed against institutionalism because it covered up social, economic, and political inequalities that could be addressed directly in a free, open, democratic public sphere. Rousseau rejected the idea that government is or ought to be a neutral arbiter, separate from the sovereign people. According to Marshall Berman, Rousseau's main contention was with the liberal state, which Berman describes as a "political mask." The masks that Rousseau saw in both royal and bourgeois culture kept people opaque to each other and kept the government opaque from people as a whole. Berman explains: "Rousseau attacked a dualistic view of state and society. The idea of a government of laws—not men—was absurd to him; all laws, after all, were made by men."[12] Hobbesian government did not encourage deliberation, action, and the practices of participatory politics, but fear. Equally important was that it was an entity wholly separate from the people it governed. This separateness was less severe and fear-based, but equally as psychically alienating in Lockean government, which existed solely to protect private property of individuals who shared nothing in common but their greed. Far from self-realization and the cultivation of community, elites only occasionally engaged in politics for the furtherance of their material prospects, while the underclasses engaged not at all.

FRENCH REVOLUTION

We spoke in our theatrical politics chapter about the ways in which French revolutionaries grew paranoid and violent over bourgeois hypocrisy. Related to this was their anti-institutionalism on behalf of the poor. The Jacobin Terror was waged on behalf of the underclass who had been left out of institutional politics. In the name of the *sans-culottes*, the Jacobins sought to upend the social inequalities that plagued France under the *ancien régime*. J.F. Bosher explains the class distinctions at work on the eve of the Revolution:

> Among the many social differences in France, the most universal and endur-
> ing was the one between all these middling and upper groups taken together,
> whom we may call the "public," and the classes whom they regarded as
> inferior and called collectively *la foule*, or *le peuple*—that is, the "masses" or
> "the populace."[13]

Bosher, no friend to the Revolutionary cause, goes on to single out Rousseau as the standout who romanticized the many poor rather than condemning them. His anti-institutionalism and his embrace of the poor are reminiscent of populists today who, either by genuine compassion or by a penchant for theatrical performance of everyman sympathies, signal their camaraderie with those the system has left behind. From this impulse often follows a caricature of the poor and downtrodden that is just as detached from lived experience as those who had characterized them as ignorant. In this way, authentic, anti-institutional politics can be extreme; it often asserts idealistic myths about classes of people that invert, rather than challenge, the prevailing myths:

> The general public assumed that 'the vulgar were, and would doubtless for-
> ever be, prey to passion and superstition; reason was beyond them.' The
> principal exception, the writer Jean-Jacques Rousseau, only escaped the pre-
> vailing views of his time by dwelling upon a utopian and utterly imaginary
> notion of the French peasant and his life.[14]

This potentially explosive gulf between "public" and "mass" is implicit in the exclusionary Lockean formulation and has given rise to many forms of radical and reactionary politics and to less noxious but still rhetorically potent populist movements. Locke's impartial political institutions treat members of the respectable public with fairness. The institutions get their legitimacy only and directly from the consent of that public. Yet in doing this, they render only those who are considered "the public" (which for Locke meant people with property) politically visible. Beginning in revolutionary France, the response of populists, of the non-institutionalized remainders, and of those who claimed to speak for them, was rage.

COUNTERREVOLUTIONARY INSTITUTIONALISM: PUBLIUS

Rousseauist visions of authenticity and joyful community were based on assumptions that the more compassionate sides of human nature could manifest themselves in politics. The unleashing of authentic compassion would create a society where individuals could exist as radically sovereign individuals. Yet they could unite into a mass identity based on their shared principles of virtue and national citizenship, rather than on their shared political institutions. This vision spawned the French Revolution. In France, shortly after ratification of the US Constitution, the politics of authenticity attempted to break down the barriers of social stratification, atomization of individuals in their daily lives, and class divisions that the Enlightenment had created. This also meant destroying established institutions and rule of law. Conservatives like Edmund Burke (who we will discuss more in depth in a later chapter) lamented these radical movements for attempting to radically transform human society away from its concrete experiences in everyday life.

While Burke was writing, American participatory democrats were advancing a politics of authenticity on their own continent. Like Rousseau and Robespierre, the Anti-Federalists sought to make the natural human trait of "virtue," not shared, impersonal institutions, the glue that would hold a self-governing polity together. As The Federal Farmer argues, "Whatever the refinement of modern politics may inculcate, it still is certain that some degree of virtue must exist, or freedom cannot live."[15] Virtue would allow citizens to empathize and cooperate with each other in public life, rather than manipulate each other. Similarly, the relationship between the representatives and the people ought to be a transparent one, held together by the bonds of mutual recognition. Melancton Smith, in debating Hamilton at the New York Ratifying Convention, argued:

> The idea that naturally suggests itself to our minds, when we speak of representatives is, that they resemble those they represent; they should be a true picture of the people; possess the knowledge of their circumstances and their wants; sympathize in all their distresses, and be disposed to seek their true interests.[16]

But counterrevolutionary pessimism about human nature in the United States figured heavily in the construction of the American Constitution, with its stable, complex, and somewhat depoliticizing institutions. Considering the repulsion that the gentry class of the United States felt toward these radical ideas in the 1780s, it is no wonder why Shay's Rebellion, in which debt-ridden farmers in western Massachusetts revolted against the government, was a major catalyst for the constitutional convention. Emotional self-expression, the attempted leveling of social classes, and reliance on public virtue central to the politics of authenticity were seen as anathema to liberty and to the peaceful resolution of grievances through institutions. The American Constitution was meant to avoid these emotional outbursts and calls for egalitarian virtues among the populace. As Madison relays in "Federalist 49": "it is the reason, alone, of the public, that ought to control and regulate the government. The passions ought to be controlled and regulated by the government."[17] As Daniel Walker Howe describes, "any such revised attitude toward the passions was alien to Publius; if it was a revolution, he was a counterrevolutionary."[18]

To the horror of many of the more radical American revolutionaries like Thomas Paine, *The Federalist Papers* repeatedly taper the transparency between citizens and between citizens and government. Madison makes the argument that Rousseauist-style pure democracy is dangerous because it destroys individual liberty:

> Democracies have ever been spectacles of turbulence and contention; have ever been found incompatible with personal security or the rights of property; and have in general been as short in their lives as they have been violent in their deaths.[19]

The Federalists argued that direct democracy, rather than creating avenues for virtue and mutual compassion, bound individuals together into unthinking mobs. In "Federalist 55", Madison argues that when individuals unite for political purposes, even the wisest lose their ability to think independently: "In all very numerous assemblies, of whatever character composed, passion never fails to wrest the sceptre from reason. Had every Athenian citizen been a Socrates, every Athenian assembly would still have been a mob."[20] To avoid mobs, Madison prescribes "THE TOTAL EXCLUSION OF THE PEOPLE, IN THEIR COLLECTIVE CAPACITY, from any share" in governmental power.[21] In the places and times of Rousseau, Thoreau, America in the 1960s, and Trumpism in the late 2010s, this formulation would have been politically unfeasible.

Madison's corrective for the type of social intimacy, and the mass identity that Arendt claimed followed it, is the idea of a large commercial republic with many factions, where citizens will be virtually unable to empathize and unite on political causes. Madison was anticipating something important here. The revolutionaries on the left and reactionaries on the right in the nineteenth and twentieth centuries mobilized the masses toward revolutionary goals by giving them unitary identities, so that citizens identified with one another, typically by using rousing, emotional, nationalistic language. The Jacobins relied on a republican national identity to push their revolutionary agenda. Karl Marx urged *workers* of the world to unite in order to throw off their chains. Communist and fascist totalitarian parties relied on the unitary identity of class or race, in to advance their march toward an inevitable national destiny. Martin Diamond showed how Publius had warded of revolutionary Marxism in particular. In a section called "Madison versus Marx," Diamond argues:

> Madison anticipated and refuted Marxism. Rather than compacting into two distinct great classes, in Madison's theory, rich and poor are fragmented and jumbled together into narrow and particular "factions." Accordingly, no single owning class oppresses the masses; and the masses do not organize as a class, but rather fragment and factionally advance specialized, immediate interests. This is just what happened. One of the remarkable features of American politics is the absence of powerful Marxist movements like those in Western Europe.[22]

Indeed, Madison rejected Rousseau's conjecture that property and commerce were not natural to mankind in its original state and instead ventured that class identity would divide free citizens into factions:

> The latent causes of faction are thus sown in the nature of man; and we see them everywhere brought into different degrees of activity, according to the different circumstances of civil society ... So strong is the propensity of mankind to fall into mutual animosities that where no substantial occasion presents itself the most frivolous and fanciful distinctions have been sufficient to kindle their unfriendly passions and excite their most violent conflicts. But the most common and durable source of factions has been the various and unequal distribution of property. This who hold and those who are without property have ever formed distinct interests in society.[23]

Thus, inverting Marx, Madison attempted to prevent mass consciousness-building.

The sheer size and complexity of the new nation would weaken class solidarity, which the Rousseauists would clearly denote as alienating. The

plan for a large, commercial republic that would prevent too much camaraderie among the citizenship is found in "Federalist 10." Madison suggests that depoliticization will lead to citizens remaining opaque from one
another:

> Extend the sphere, and you take in a greater variety of parties and interests;
> you make it less probable that a majority of the whole will have a common
> motive to invade the rights of other citizens; or if such a common motive
> exists, it will be more difficult for all who feel it to discover their own
> strength, and to act in unison with each other. Besides other impediments,
> it may be remarked that, where there is a consciousness of unjust or dishon-
> orable purposes, communication is always checked by distrust in proportion
> to the number whose concurrence is necessary.[24]

The Federalists believed that too much cohesiveness within identity
groups, or too much camaraderie and closeness among citizens, would
frustrate independent thought. A politics of authenticity would not lead to
a celebratory public realm in which citizens expressed themselves and
identified with others. Rather than cultivating love and trust among citizens, too much closeness would unleash hatred and suspicion. The formal
institutions and processes the Federalists promoted would seek to solve
any pressing social problems in a slow, deliberate manner while maintaining a proper opacity between citizens, and between the citizenry and its
representatives.

So on the one hand, we see the conditions for a *lack* of mass identity in
the minds of citizens. Institutionally, we also see the conditions built for
concurrent or even sometimes *conflicting* political identities in their minds.
Revolutionaries tend to seek one unitary identity affixing itself to the class
or the nation, whereby the people as a whole can then control their government. Madison wishes instead for multiple identities that affix themselves to many minority factions, none of which will be able to govern the
country as a whole, thus creating the need for institutions, "auxiliary precautions" to govern Americans instead:

> A dependence on the people is, no doubt, the primary control on the gov-
> ernment; but experience has taught mankind the necessity of auxiliary pre-
> cautions ... This policy of supplying, by opposite and rival interests, the
> defect of better motives, might be traced through the whole system of
> human affairs, private as well as public.[25]

Far from making the people their own sovereign, undivided governors, Madison then goes on to divide the legislature of American government into two:

> In republican government, the legislative authority necessarily predominates. The remedy for this inconveniency is to divide the legislature into different branches; and to render them, by different modes of election and different principles of action, as little connected with each other as the nature of their common functions and their common dependence on the society will admit.[26]

Here, we see that human nature is not a reliable or stable ground upon which to build a large political society, and that many concurrent identities and institutions are needed to thwart mass democracy.

Assigning Americans different loyalties is also reflected in the specific design of American federalism, by giving citizens different levels of government with which to identify. Americans, according to the Federalists, would split their identities between many different fraternal loyalties by holding diverse factional attachments, especially in the economic realm. As citizens, they would split their political identities between different forms of government. One way in which *The Federalist* suggests this diversity is in "Federalist 39," when Madison discusses whether the states or the American people created the constitution:

> [I]t appears, on one hand, that the Constitution is to be founded on the assent and ratification of the people of America, given by deputies elected for the special purpose; but, on the other, that this assent and ratification is to be given by the people, not as individuals composing one entire nation, but as composing the distinct and independent States to which they respectively belong. It is to be the assent and ratification of the several States, derived from the supreme authority in each State, the authority of the people themselves. The act, therefore, establishing the Constitution, will not be a NATIONAL, but a FEDERAL act.[27]

By splitting American political identities between state and federal levels, this would further prevent the development of a mass identity.

Any counterrevolutionary project would not be sufficient without reliance on elites to station the institutions of government. Madison tells us in "Federalist 35": "The idea of an actual representation of all classes of the people, by persons of each class, is altogether visionary."[28] Daniel Walker Howe describes:

> Most political representatives in the new government would and should be large landowners, merchants, or professional men. If a single social group could be identified as impartial, it was the professionals, who were not tied to any particular property interest as the landowners and merchants were. The short-sighted masses were not likely to look after the interests of society as well as these other groups.[29]

A reliance on a pluralism among elite representatives, as they battled with each other seemingly on behalf of their constituents, would prevent ordinary citizens, illiterate in the ways of legal and constitutional formalisms, from using the government for their passionate ends. These elite representatives would station the legislative, executive, and judicial branches as defenders of the public good. Over time in the United States, they would establish the slow, stable, deliberative processes that would keep social change moving slowly.

ANTI-INSTITUTIONALISM

The ideas of Hobbes, Locke, Montesquieu, and Madison became prominent during a time before universal suffrage, and before the inclusivity that excluded persons demanded in public life. Jürgen Habermas tells us that the early "bourgeois public sphere" was a free and open space of equals who could debate and negotiate rationally on the issues and problems of the day. According to Habermas, there were "institutional criteria" in this sphere that governed social intercourse. One was "the disregard of rank" so that individuals could speak freely, and openly, where "the better argument could assert itself." Another was the idea of "inclusivity" in the public. Either through direct presentation or *re*-presentation, a broad "public" and its concerns were valid in the realm of politics and were seen as having the ability to participate in politics, directly or indirectly. Habermas argues:

> However exclusive the public might be in any given instance, it could never close itself off entirely and become consolidated as a clique ...[t]he issues discussed became more 'general' not merely in their significance, but also in their accessibility: everyone had to be able to participate. Wherever the public established itself institutionally as a stable group of discussants, it did not

equate itself with the public but at most claimed to act as its mouthpiece, in its name, perhaps even as its educator—the new form of bourgeois representation.[30]

For Habermas, the legislative bodies of the liberal world were meant to be spaces of representation and access for a public composed of private persons who could debate and compromise on their concerns.

Feminist scholar Nancy Fraser takes issue with Habermas's idea that the bourgeois public sphere disregarded rank (and therefore, the power relations that go along with it) that allowed for easy access and entry into politics. Like for Rousseau, the idea that the institutions of governmental could somehow be separated from social life, with all its inequalities, was impossible:

> Liberal political theory assumes that it is possible to organize a democratic form of political life on the basis of socio-economic and socio-sexual structures that generate systemic inequalities. For liberals, then, the problem of democracy becomes the problem of how to insulate political processes from what are considered to be non-political or pre-political processes, those characteristic, for example, of the economy, the family, and informal everyday life. The problem for liberals, thus, is how to separate the barriers separating political institutions that are supposed to instantiate relations of equality from economic, cultural, and socio-sexual institutions that are premised on systemic relations of inequality.[31]

We see here with Fraser that liberal institutionalists do not merely fail to create conditions for inclusivity into politics, but that they actively must suppress outside voices in order to maintain their hegemony.

Not only do seemingly neutral institutions often discriminate against those on the lower end of the social hierarchies in terms of racial, gender, or class identities, but they also can prevent simple, pragmatic legislation from becoming law that are seeming free of identity politics. In 1995, after Bill Clinton failed to pass comprehensive healthcare reform, Sven Steinmo and Jon Watts wrote a paper entitled "It's the Institutions, Stupid! Why Comprehensive National Health Insurance Always Fails in America." In it, they point not merely to recent institutional blockages to healthcare reform, but the fragmented federal system that the United States has had going back to the founding, as detailed in *The Federalist Papers*.[32] It is no wonder then that the Affordable Care Act of 2010 required a great deal of institutional maneuvering, lamented by conservatives.

More importantly, the idea and practice of elitist pluralism in the United States has always come with a large degree of exclusion of various persons from the original constitutional order. The liberal idea of a nation of governance through impersonal institutions, of "laws not men," as Rousseau lamented, meant that social inequalities were left intact and that the elitism of the social world was simply transformed into political elitism, thus strengthening these inequalities in both realms. The working classes, women, and enslaved persons were done a disservice by the constitutional ambiguity about citizenship. The structure of American institutions in *The Federalist* created multiple identities for Americans between national, state, local levels, and between factional interests as a way to avoid mass identity and create stability. This was a philosophical preference of Madison, who envisioned a dynamic, pluralistic public sphere, at least for those who could access power. But the pragmatic considerations of elites in the 1780 also led to enshrine ambiguous political identities in political institutions. As Rogers Smith points out, at the founding, "[i]ssues of state versus national identity and slavery, especially, were so explosive that the framers avoided raising them whenever possible and left them largely unresolved."[33] As a result, Rogers argues, this set the stage for the political realm to constitutionally deny the rights of citizenship to various groups of people over the ensuing years.

Through law, custom, and access to power limited to elites, institutional politics, in the minds of radicals and progressive reformers, has often led to exclusion and injustice, either real or perceived, from various "forgotten" groups in America. The realities of being "left out" of the civic arena prompted occluded groups and individuals to engage in politics outside the realm of formal institutions: radical authentic politics, performative, attention-drawing politics, or a combination of both. The politics of autobiography was prevalent in the abolitionist movements of the 1830s–1860s; feminist movements of both the nineteenth and twentieth centuries relied on personal grievances to advance their causes into the institutional arena. These mostly leftist movements have often reflected Rousseauist notions of merging the personal with the political, and the social with the institutional, which late eighteenth-century American liberalism had failed to do. In the 2010s, we are seeing a resurgence of these anti-institutional politics, particularly on the right. This is an issue to which will return when we explore the co-opting of anti-institutionalist sentiment and rhetoric on the populist right.

TOWARD THE CRISIS OF THE CIVIL WAR

The failure of institutions often sets the stage for radicalism, both in the form of extreme authentic politics and extreme theatrical politics. This is especially true when those institutions purport to be moral neutral and objective, yet they enshrine and calcify the existing power hierarchies in society. This was the tension leading to the American Civil War. Abraham Lincoln assumed the presidency while the nation was coming apart over slavery, without any obvious institutional mechanisms to assuage conflicts. As Rogers Smith puts it:

> The nature of American citizenship became the legal focal point for the nation's increasingly unbearable conflicts over the kind of political economy that would prevail as the nation expanded westward, over the primacy of state or national power on a wide range of issues, and especially over whether America would be officially defined as a white man's nation rather than a union dedicated to human moral equality and individual rights.

For Smith, the calcified institutionalization of racial exclusion created "constitutional chains" for African Americans like Dred Scott. In a legal sense, the country was divided, since the south was about to secede from the Union. But it was also true in the political sense, between proslavery and anti-slavery voices, between racists and non-racists, and within the group of opponents to chattel slavery, since some were clamoring for its immediate, sometimes lawlessly violent, overthrow, while others were urging patience, moderation, and incrementalism.

The most notorious and violently radical abolitionist was John Brown, who, as we noted in the last chapter, Henry David Thoreau had defended with theatrical flourish. In October of 1859, Brown and several other men seized an armory at Harpers Ferry, West Virginia, for the purpose of arming slaves for a violent insurrection against their masters. In his final speech, Brown invokes a central tenet in Rousseauist, Platonist truth-telling authenticity: the sacrificing of one's corporal well-being in the service of the downtrodden:

> Now, if it is deemed necessary that I should forfeit my life for the further-ance of the ends of justice, and mingle my blood further with the blood of my children and with the blood of millions in this slave country whose rights are disregarded by wicked, cruel, and unjust enactments, I submit; so let it be done![34]

Radical abolitionist William Lloyd Garrison was the leader of the radical, yet pacifist wing of the abolitionist movement which gained steam in the 1830s, 1840s, and 1850s. He opened his first edition of *The Liberator* with an uncompromising tone:

> I am aware that many object to the severity of my language. Is there not cause for severity? I will be as harsh as truth, and as uncompromising as justice. On this subject, I do not wish to think, or to speak, or write with moderation. No, no! Tell a man whose house is on fire to give a moderate alarm! Tell him to moderately rescue his wife from the hands of a ravisher! Tell the mother to gradually extricate her babe from the fire into which it has fallen! But urge me not to use moderation in a cause like the present. I am in earnest. I will not equivocate, I will not excuse, I will not retreat a single inch! And I WILL BE HEARD![35]

Garrison's *legal* gripe stemmed from his moral outrage, and it was with what he saw as the proslavery US Constitution, which had defended slavery by including the three-fifths compromise and the fugitive slave clause. For this reason, Garrison did not vote and did not endorse political candidates or parties, since participation in electoral politics was to participate in evil institutionalist politics. This anti-constitutional, anti-institutional stance is detailed most vividly by an anti-slavery gathering in Framingham, Massachusetts, on July 4, 1854, that was called to protest the Fugitive Slave Act. Wendell Phillips, Sojourner Truth, and Henry David Thoreau all attended, but Garrison was the most vivid in his speech. Lighting a copy of the Fugitive Slave Law on fire, he shouted "And let the people say Amen" to which the crowd responded "Amen!" He then pulled out a copy of the US Constitution, called it "the parent of all the other atrocities ... A covenant with death ... An agreement with hell," and then set it on fire continuing to shout "so perish all compromises with tyranny! And let the people say Amen" to which the crowd again shouted "Amen!"[36]

Not all anti-slavery voices were violent or anti-institutionalist, but were still rhetorically scathing nonetheless. Two years prior, also on the fourth of July, Frederick Douglass attacked the hypocrisy of American exceptionalism by bringing attention to enslaved African Americans:

> What, to the American slave, is your 4th of July? I answer; a day that reveals to him, more than all other days in the year, the gross injustice and cruelty to which he is the constant victim. To him, your celebration is a sham; your boasted liberty, an unholy license; your national greatness, swelling vanity;

your sounds of rejoicing are empty and heartless; your denunciation of tyrants, brass fronted impudence; your shouts of liberty and equality, hollow mockery; your prayers and hymns, your sermons and thanksgivings, with all your religious parade and solemnity are, to Him, mere bombast, fraud, deception, impiety, and hypocrisy—a thin veil to cover up crimes which would disgrace a nation of savages. There is not a nation on earth guilty of practices more shocking and bloody than are the people of the United States at this very hour ....[37]

Here, we see moral truth-telling from Douglass, who was speaking not merely from the perspective of an orator, but from personal biography. This mode of address aligns with a Rousseauist politics of authenticity, under which speakers speak not with the prejudices of audiences in mind, but from one's unique personal experience of injustice, in order to shake listeners from their moral complacency. Yet while Douglass spoke outside the bounds of polite society in his denunciation of American hypocrisy, however, he was an institutionalist. Unlike Garrison, Douglass believed firstly that slavery could be abolished while the constitutional system held intact and, secondly, that voting for anti-slavery politicians and political parties (like the Free Soil Party, and even the more morally ambiguous Republican Party) could lead to slavery's demise:

[The Garrisonians] hold the Constitution to be a slaveholding instrument, and will not cast a vote or hold office, and denounce all who vote or hold office, no matter how faithfully such persons labour to promote the abolition of slavery. I, on the other hand, deny that the Constitution guarantees the right to hold property in man, and believe that the way to abolish slavery in America is to vote such men into power as well use their powers for the abolition of slavery.[38]

ABRAHAM LINCOLN: MORAL INSTITUTIONALIST

Lincoln had long been an opponent of slavery in both private and public, although he did not consider himself an "abolitionist" in the radical sense of the word. The reason for which Lincoln is so justly celebrated is his success in emancipation, yet his theatrical, performative political skills and legal moderation in an era of radical authentic truth-telling and disregard for law is what makes him worth celebrating. Ralph Waldo Emerson spoke in a speech after Lincoln's assassination of Lincoln's political ability to speak to different audiences without exposing his inner intentions:

His broad good humor, running easily into jocular talk, in which he delighted and in which he excelled, was a rich gift to this wise man. It enabled him to keep his secret; to meet every kind of man and every rank in society; to take off the edge of the severest decisions; to mask his own purpose and sound his companion; and to catch with true instinct the temper of every company he addressed.

Unlike the stoic truth-teller of Rousseau's imagination Lincoln, then, was a political virtuoso who could shape-shift within the maelstrom of public life without revealing himself. This was required within the context of a pluralistic, factuous political system like the United States in the mid-nineteenth century. Thoreau and Lincoln both relied on silent contemplation at times in order to rediscover the moral truths to which they were dedicated. Yet while Thoreau's theatrical prophesy required him to work outside the accepted channels of politics, Lincoln worked from the inside.

Early in Lincoln's career, we find an institutionalist appeal to the rule of law that the architects of the politics of authenticity would have considered artificial window-dressing. In his 1838 *Address Before the Young Men's Lyceum of Springfield Illinois*, Lincoln laments the increasing mob violence taking place in the southern states and, with great rhetorical flourish, lauds the adherence to law as a tribute to the founding fathers:

Let every American, every lover of liberty, every well wisher to his posterity, swear by the blood of the Revolution, never to violate in the least particular, the laws of the country; and never to tolerate their violation by others. As the patriots of seventy-six did to the support of the Declaration of Independence, so to the support of the Constitution and Laws, let every American pledge his life, his property, and his sacred honor;—let every man remember that to violate the law, is to trample on the blood of his father, and to tear the character of his own, and his children's liberty. Let reverence for the laws, be breathed by every American mother, to the lisping babe, that prattles on her lap—let it be taught in schools, in seminaries, and in colleges; let it be written in Primers, spelling books, and in Almanacs;—let it be preached from the pulpit, proclaimed in legislative halls, and enforced in courts of justice. And, in short, let it become the political religion of the nation; and let the old and the young, the rich and the poor, the grave and the gay, of all sexes and tongues, and colors and conditions, sacrifice unceasingly upon its altars.[39]

Here, we see Lincoln the institutionalist. Logically, if Lincoln only believed in institutionalist politics through regular order, legal institutions like slavery would be allowed to flourish forever, as long as majorities agreed to it. Yet, Harry Jaffa notes in his seminal work *Crisis of the House Divided*, by subtly shrugging off some forms of mob action against bad individuals, Lincoln subtly suggests that we ought to not merely follow the law, but work toward good law:

> Those who believe anything sanctioned by law is right commit one great error; those who believe the law should sanction only what is right commit another. Either error might result in foolish laws; and, although a foolish law may be preferable to a wise dictator, a wise law is preferable to both.[40]

Here, we see Lincoln attempting to resolve the tension between the politics of authenticity and its demand for direct, moral truth-telling, Garrisonian theatrical politics, which demands shocking the consciences of audiences, and institutional politics, which asks us to leave our uncompromising moralism at the door and follow the law no matter what the ethical compromises.

Lincoln is doing something similar to Thoreau here, but using the law, rather than the natural language of poetry, as his communicative foundation with his audience. He is urging his listeners to follow the law, but also to work to change unjust law so that it becomes more aligned with their consciences. As in Thoreau's poetical communication, this is subtle, suggestive, and lacks the authoritarianism of a hegemonic profit. Whereas Thoreau is asking us to rediscover *nature* alongside him as we think about how to act in the world, Lincoln is asking us to rediscover our *institutions*, fortified through a shared *history* as we do the same. In both cases, speaker and audience rediscover moral truths with some distance between them, and with some personal depth to their thinking.

What follows in Lincoln's career are a series of subtle advances toward moral law, following along the outer confines of the legal structure that already existed in the constitution. These advances require Lincoln, as Emerson lauded, to conceal his own designs on American constitutional law, or on the institution of slavery. Like Thoreau, Lincoln seeks to create an elusiveness and a psychic distance between him and his listeners, rather than an intimate, shared space of empathy for each other's inner selves, as Rousseau imagined in his directly democratic society. His incrementalism prevents him from demanding politically immediate solutions to moral problems. In his famous "House Divided Speech" in 1858, Lincoln does present a radical vision for the country, when he posits that the nation will either be all slave or all free. Yet, he does so with an important qualifying word that separates him from the radical abolitionists led by Garrison, who wish to see the constitutional order replaced with a morally righteous order: "I believe this government cannot endure, *permanently* half slave and half free" [emphasis added].

Shortly after Lincoln's election, many southerners were arguing that their states had a right to leave the Union since they had voluntarily joined it in 1789 based on the stipulation that slavery would be protected. Lincoln eludes this problem in his First Inaugural Address, which is largely addressed to the south. He suggests that while the constitution is important, it is not the only legal document upon which American law has been based:

> in legal contemplation the Union is perpetual confirmed by the history of the Union itself. The Union is much older than the Constitution. It was formed, in fact, by the Articles of Association in 1774. It was matured and continued by the Declaration of Independence in 1776. It was further matured, and the faith of all the then thirteen States expressly plighted and engaged that it should be perpetual, by the Articles of Confederation in 1778. And finally, in 1787, one of the declared objects for ordaining and establishing the Constitution was 'to form a more perfect Union.'

This opens space for Lincoln to elevate the significance of the Declaration of Independence, which up until that point had been more of a partisan document than a nationally revered credo. The Declaration had always had significance for Lincoln. In his 1857 "Speech on the Dred Scott Decision," Lincoln offered the following:

> I think the authors of that notable instrument intended to include all men, but they did not intend to declare all men equal in all respects. They did not mean to say all were equal in color, size, intellect, moral developments, or social capacity. They defined with tolerable distinctness, in what respects they did consider all men created equal-equal in "certain inalienable rights, among which are life, liberty, and the pursuit of happiness." This they said, and this meant. They did not mean to assert the obvious untruth, that all were then actually enjoying that equality, nor yet, that they were about to confer it immediately upon them. In fact they had no power to confer such a boon. They meant simply to declare the right, so that the enforcement of it might follow as fast as circumstances should permit. They meant to set up a standard maxim for free society, which should be familiar to all, and revered by

all; constantly looked to, constantly labored for, and even though never perfectly attained, constantly approximated, and thereby constantly spreading and deepening its influence, and augmenting the happiness and value of life to all people of all colors everywhere. The assertion that 'all men are created equal' was of no practical use in effecting our separation from Great Britain; and it was placed in the Declaration, nor for that, but for future use.[41]

Finally, we can look to the Gettysburg Address as the most theatrical of all of Lincoln's writings. According to Garry Wills, the Gettysburg Address gave new meaning to the Declaration by elevating it to the status of a constitution.

Lincoln performed one of the most daring acts of open-air sleight-of-hand ever witnessed by the unsuspecting. Everyone in that vast throng of thousands was having his or her intellectual pocket picked. The crowd departed with a new thing in its ideological luggage, that new constitution Lincoln had substituted or the one they brought there with them. They walked off, from those curving graves on the hillside, under hanged sky, into a different America. Lincoln had revolutionized the Revolution, giving people a new past to live that would change their future indefinitely.[42]

Here, we see for Lincoln, the same culmination of the process Thoreau experienced: reaching a transformative prophetic message after much personal introspection, away from the crowd. By invoking biblical allegories in the Gettysburg Address (which whiz audience must have recognized), Lincoln establishes, as Thoreau did for Stanley Cavell, as a "visible saint" at *Walden*, his right to transform the man-made constitutional order.

CONCLUSION

The preceding interpretation of Lincoln is the one most often retold by conservatives: Lincoln, the slow, steady institutionalist, refusing to cave to the demands of radical abolitionists, employing tactful, performative rhetoric to navigate his way around institutions. Appeals to the "party of Lincoln" have been made by the more moderate members of the Republican Party in recent decades, especially when courting the votes of people of color. Yet there have also always been strains of reactionary conservatism which seek not to slow, moderate, or guide progress, but to reverse social gains using raw emotion and directness of address. Since the 1960s, these populist voices have become more prominent. Rather than finding a strategic and moral balance between authenticity, theatricality, and institutional constraints that modify the extremes of both, Trumpian conservatism has become *the* anti-institutional ideology in the United States. We will explore this phenomenon in the next chapter.

NOTES

1. Jane Monica Drexler, "Politics Improper: Iris Marion Young, Hannah Arendt, and the Power of Performativity." *Hypatia* 22:4 (2007), 4.
2. Aristotle, *Politics*, trans. Ernest Barker (Oxford: Oxford University Press, 1998), 200.
3. Aristotle, *Politics*, 34.
4. Thomas Hobbes, "Of Commonwealth," from *Leviathan* in *Classics of Modern Political Theory*, ed. Steven M. Cahn (Oxford: Oxford University Press, 1997), 136.
5. John Locke, "Of the Ends of Political Society and Government," from *The Second Treatise of Civil Government* in *Classics of Modern Political Theory*, ed. Steven M. Cahn (Oxford: Oxford University Press, 1997), 254.
6. Locke *The Second Treatise*, 257.
7. Locke *The Second Treatise*, 259.
8. Bruce Ackerman, "Good-Bye Montesquieu" in *Comparative Administrative Law*, ed. Susan Rose-Ackerman and Peter L. Lindseth (Edward Elgar, 2013), 128.
9. Charles-Louis de Secondat, Baron de Montesquieu, "Of the Constitution of England," from *The Spirit of the Laws* in *Classics of Modern Political Theory*, ed. Steven M. Cahn (Oxford: Oxford University Press, 1997), 347.
10. Marshall Berman, *The Politics of Authenticity: Radical Individualism and the Emergence of Modern Society* (London: Verso, 2009), 120.
11. Berman, *The Politics of Authenticity*, 121.
12. Berman, *The Politics of Authenticity*, 120.
13. J.F. Bosher, *The French Revolution* (New York: Norton, 1989), 31.
14. Bosher, *The French Revolution*, 32.
15. A Federal Republican, "A Review of the Constitution Proposed by the Late Convention" in *The Complete Anti-Federalist*, eds. Herbert J. Storing, and Murray Dry (Chicago: University of Chicago, 2008), 76.
16. Melancton Smith, "Speech at the New York Ratifying Convention," in *Classics of American Political and Constitutional Thought*, eds. Scott J. Hammond, Kevin R. Hardwick, and Howard L. Lubert (Indianapolis: Hackett Pub., 2007), 581.
17. Publius, "Federalist 49" in *The Federalist Papers*, ed. Clinton Rossiter (New York: Signet Classic, 2003), 314.

18. Daniel Walker Howe, *Making the American Self Jonathan Edwards to Abraham Lincoln* (Oxford: Oxford University Press, 2009), 84.
19. Publius, "Federalist 10," 76.
20. Publius, "Federalist 10," 340.
21. Publius, "Federalist 10," 385.
22. Martin Diamond, *The Founding of the Democratic Republic* (Wadsworth Publishing Company, 1998), 73.
23. Publius, "Federalist 10," 73–74.
24. Publius, "Federalist 10," 78.
25. Publius, "Federalist 51," 319.
26. Publius, "Federalist 51," 319.
27. Publius, "Federalist 39," 239.
28. Publius, "Federalist 39," 210.
29. Howe, *Making the American Self*, 88.
30. Jürgen Habermas, *The Structural Transformation of the Public Sphere: An Inquiry into a Category of Bourgeois Society*, trans. Thomas Burger (London: Polity, 1989), 37.
31. Nancy Fraser, "Rethinking the Public Sphere: A Contribution to the Critique of Actually Existing Democracy," *Social Text* 25, no. 26 (1990): 56–80.
32. Sven Steinmo and Jon Watts, "It's the Institutions, Stupid! Why Comprehensive National Health Insurance Always Fails in America," *Journal of Health Politics, Policy and Law* 20, no. 2 (Summer 1995).
33. Rogers M. Smith, *Civic Ideals: Conflicting Visions of Citizenship in U.S. History* (New Haven: Yale University Press, 1999), 116.
34. John Brown, "John Brown's Last Speech," History is a Weapon, Accessed March 15, 2018, http://www.historyisaweapon.com/defcon1/john-brown.html.
35. William Lloyd Garrison, "To The Public" (January 1, 1831) from *The Liberator*, https://www.pbs.org/wgbh/aia/part4/4h2928t.html.
36. Albert B. Saye, "A Covenant With Death: An Essay-Review," *The Georgia Historical Quarterly* 59, no. 3 (1975): 330.
37. Frederick Douglass, "Fourth of July Oration" (1852), in Political Thought in America, ed. Michael B. Levy (Waveland Press, 1992), 267.
38. Frederick Douglass, "The Constitution of the United States: Is it Pro-Slavery or Anti-Slavery?" (March 26, 1860), Black Past, http://www.blackpast.org/1860-frederick-douglass-constitution-united-states-it-pro-slavery-or-anti-slavery.
39. Abraham Lincoln, "Address to the Young Man's Lyceum of Springfield, Illinois" (1838), in Political Thought in America, ed. Michael B. Levy (Waveland Press, 1992), 267.

40. Harry V. Jaffa, *Crisis of the House Divided: an Interpretation of the Issues in the Lincoln-Douglas Debates* (University of Chicago Press, 1982), 195.

41. Abraham Lincoln, "Speech on the Dred Scott Decision" (1857) in *American Political Thought*, ed. Kenneth M. Dolbeare (Chatham, NJ: Chatham House, 1998), 281.

42. Garry Wills, *Lincoln at Gettysburg: The Words That Remade America* (New York: Simon and Schuster, 1992), 38.

CHAPTER 6

How the Right Co-opted Anti-institutionalism

In 2016, Donald Trump defeated sixteen other candidates running for the Republican nomination. This was despite the fact that Trump, according to his Republican rivals, was not a conservative. He had bucked Republican orthodoxy on issues of trade, foreign policy, healthcare, abortion, and others. The few policies that Trump promised to enact during the primaries and into the general election were seen as largely symbolic. Even most of Trump's supporters, when asked, did not believe that his proposal to build a wall along the border of Mexico, for example, was possible.[1] By the final weeks of the general election, neither he, his opponent, nor the media discussed Trump's issue stances much at all. In three presidential debates, the topic of deportations was barely addressed.[2] From the primaries to the general election, Trump's campaign was not about issues, but about the character, temperament, and authenticity of Trump in relation to the other candidates.

What set Trump apart from the rest of the Republican field was not necessarily his challenge to the Republican Party on issues, nor his more hardline stances on immigration, but his lack of decorum and straightforward speaking style. A poll released in December 2015 showed that 71% of Republicans believed that Trump "tells it like it is."[3] In the South Carolina Primary, which Trump won, 78% of those who said that this was the top quality they are looking for in a candidate voted for Trump.[4] Far and away, the core of Trump's appeal to the populist wing of the Republican Party was that he was willing to take on what is seen as an oppressive culture of

© The Author(s) 2019
D. J. McCool, *Three Frames of Modern Politics*,
https://doi.org/10.1007/978-3-319-95648-0_6

political correctness. This appeal was first featured with his lambasting of Megyn Kelly at a Fox News debate on March 3, 2016, when she suggested that the ways he had spoken about women were inappropriate. After lobbing an insult at Rosie O'Donnell, Trump explained, to great applause, "I think the big problem this country has is being politically correct. I've been challenged by so many people, and I don't frankly have time for political correctness. And to be honest with you, this country doesn't have time either." Trump and his surrogates used his anti-political correctness stance to defend his numerous controversial comments for the duration of the campaign. As time went on, however, the veneer that fighting political correctness for the sake of addressing real political problems was gone. What his supporters wanted was not a problem solver, but someone who would offend "the establishment" no matter what the electoral cost. Political attention had been moved from the concrete, physical world of policy, and into the murky, abstract world of cultural grievance, with its contests over who is considered to be an "authentic" or real American, based not on their institutional commitments, but on the forthrightness of their speech.

It is important to keep in mind that the politics of authenticity does not dictate that one speaks the truth, but that one says what one thinks or feels. Recently, the focus on this kind of personal expression of grievances has become a central feature of the reactionary, populist right more than within any other ideological subgroup in American politics. This was not always the case. The left's push for revolution and reform since the Enlightenment had sought to make "the personal political," as the 1960s feminist slogan went. The idea of that political debate ought to center on citizens' personal experiences and identities comes from the politics of authenticity. In this chapter, we'll look at the ways in which American conservatism, as a mixture of Burkean traditionalism and Lockean rationalism, has traditionally opposed authentic politics. Then, we'll explore the ways in which the populist, reactionary wing of American conservatism has gradually co-opted many elements of the politics of authenticity from the left. This has led to a state of political dysfunction in both conservatism and American politics in general that may endure for a long time.

BURKEAN CONSERVATISM

Modern conservatism began as a reaction against utopian, Rousseauist radicalism on the left. It has tended to emphasize the importance of impersonal institutions and processes in political life rather than the personalities and characters of individuals that Rousseauists emphasize. Further, modern conservatism has always countered the type of unrealistic radical utopianism that they claim leftist romantics envision in their political prescriptions. As Roger Scruton wrote in *The Meaning of Conservatism*, conservatives are "unable … to appeal to a utopian future, or to a future that is not … already contained in the present and past."[5]

Edmund Burke founded modern conservatism as a reaction to the Rousseau-inspired French Revolution. Once social masks, established institutions, and the artificial mannerisms and customs of social and political life were evaporated, warned Burke, the result would not be compassion, togetherness, and the spreading of rights to disadvantaged citizens as Rousseau had envisioned, but rage, discord, and the stifling of rights for all. Burke believed that calls for social demasking from revolutionaries like Rousseau and Thomas Paine in America would lead to chaos:

> [Now] all is to be changed. All the pleasing illusions that made power gentle, and obedience liberal, which harmonized the different shades of lie are to be dissolved by this new conquering empire of light and reason. All the decent drapery of life is to be rudely torn off. All the super-added ideas, which the heart owns, and the understanding ratifies, as necessary to cover the defects of our weak and shivering nature, and to raise it to a dignity in our own estimation, are to be exploded as a ridiculous, absurd and antiquated fashion … The age of chivalry is gone; that of sophisters, economists, and calculators has succeeded, and the glory of Europe is extinguished forever. Never, never more, shall we behold that generous loyalty to rank and sex, that proud submission, that dignified obedience, that subordination of the heart, which kept alive, even in servitude itself, the spirit of an exalted freedom.[6]

We see here an interesting debate over "nakedness" in the modern world. For revolutionaries like Rousseau and Marx, the stripping away of costumes and artifice was the way toward liberation. For Burke, primitive, unfiltered human nature is brutal, not compassionate. Social costumes, customs, and roles exist to subdue our nature. But Burke and his conservative brethren thought that the stripping away was what led to brutality. As John Adams, in his Burkean fashion, said about the French Revolution: "Rousseau preached to the French nation liberty, till they made them the most mechanical slaves; equality, till they destroyed all equity; humanity, till they became weasels and African panthers; and fraternity, till they cut one another's throats like Roman gladiators."[7] Freedom, for Burkeans, is not detachment from "rank" or "sex" or any other category that defines the individual externally, but the assumption of those roles itself. To assume otherwise is to adopt a philosophy of dangerous licentiousness.

The mass disrobing of social costumes was accompanied, for Burke, by a belief that complex problems could be solved immediately and easily, by designing exact solutions in the mind of social engineers. The lack of acknowledgment that politics was complex came to define Burkean conservatism as a reaction to the simple solutions asserted by radicals. Burke warns us of their dangerous designs:

> The science of constructing a commonwealth, or renovating it, or reforming it, is, like every other experimental science, not to be taught *a priori*. Nor is it a short experience that can instruct us in that practical science, because the real effects of moral causes are not always immediate; but that which in the first instance is prejudicial may be excellent in its remoter operation, and its excellence may arise even from the ill effects it produces in the beginning. The reverse also happens: and very plausible schemes, with very pleasing commencements, have often shameful and lamentable conclusions ... The science of government being therefore so practical in itself and intended for such practical purposes—a matter which requires experience, and even more experience than any person can gain in his whole life, however sagacious and observing he may be—it is with infinite caution that any man ought to venture upon pulling down an edifice which has answered in any tolerable degree for ages the common purposes of society, or on building it up again without having models and patterns of approved utility before his eyes.[8]

For Burke, schemes for social arrangements that were imagined before, or outside of concrete social relations, and without reference to historical precedent, were illegitimate. The idealistic visions of Plato and Rousseau, while containing "very pleasing commencements," were too far outside of experience to be useful or advisable. Hence, one of the main problems for radicals, according to Burkean conservatives, is that ideas are not grounded in experience, but abstract truths; they pertain a "hidden" human nature, or an inevitable march toward a future progress that will uncover that nature, leading to a radically different society.

Like Kateb, Thoreau, and the other theorists we encountered earlier, Burke also urges us to embrace the indeterminacy of both private identity and our place in the social realm with others:

> Dark and inscrutable are the ways by which we come into the world. The instincts which give rise to this mysterious process of nature are not of our

making. But out of physical causes, unknown to us, perhaps unknowable, arise moral duties, which, as we are able perfectly to comprehend, we are bound indispensably to perform.[9]

Burke here seems to anticipate, and warn against, the totalitarian movements of the twentieth century, which, according to Arendt, attempted to impose stability of identity in the face of anomie, and that urged the breakdown of social conventions that stood in the way of that unitary identity formation. As George Kateb prescribes, only when we can accept that the world is a "strange place" in which we are surrounded by fluctuating forces and persons not under our control can we avoid the pitfalls of totalitarian stillness. Burke seems to agree.

As mentioned in our chapter on institutional politics, the authors of *The Federalist Papers* constructed a new constitution on the counterrevolutionary idea that the personal ought not automatically be political. Madison warns of the formation of mass identities and communitarian movements, where the institutions and procedures of political society are torn down in order to placate a mass public that wants full control of its government. This tension between institutional politics and authentic politics continued into the Jacksonian Era. Suffrage rights were extended to more people, setting the conditions for more personal expression in political life and calls for reform based not on law but on personal biography. Frederick Douglass had described his experience as a slave to argue for abolition, Elizabeth Cady Stanton argued for women's rights from a domestic perspective, and Thoreau argued that politics ought to be guided not by institutional considerations and conventions but by the conscience of the self. Conservatives sought to reaffirm the founders' vision of institutional politics. Tocqueville, while he did not reject wholesale all democratic reforms, warned that in general, anti-institutionalist demands for radical equality often yielded the opposite intended consequences, stifling rights for all. As happened in his native France, the chaos that resulted from eradicating imperfect political institutions would lead to even more oppressive forms of governance:

I think that if we do not manage little by little to introduce and finally to establish democratic institutions among us, and if we abandon giving all citizens the ideas and sentiments that first prepare them for liberty and then allow them the practice of those ideas and sentiments, there will be independence for no one, neither for the bourgeois, nor for the noble, nor for the poor, nor for the rich, but an equal tyranny for all; and I foresee that if we do not succeed over time in establishing among us the peaceful dominion of the greatest number, we will arrive sooner or later at the unlimited power of one man.[10]

Proslavery traditionalists like John C. Calhoun defended institutions and traditions to restrain individuals and allow them to peacefully coexist, even as they are not equals:

We of the South will not, cannot, surrender our institutions. To maintain the existing relations between the two races, inhabiting that section of the Union, is indispensable to the peace and happiness of both. It cannot be subverted without drenching the country in blood, and extirpating one or the other of the races. Be it good or bad, slavery has grown up with our society and institutions, and is so interwoven with them that to destroy it would be to destroy us as a people.[11]

The personalization of the issue of slavery, Calhoun argues, moves history along too quickly, does away with the roles that individuals must play to keep the peace, and sets the stage for a bloody showdown between unrestrained identities. As we discussed in the last chapter, this is an instance in which rather than preventing extreme injustice institutionalism fortified and perpetuated it.

AUTHENTICITY IN THE TWENTIETH CENTURY

Edmund Burke's warning of unfiltered political expression lasted well into the twentieth century in the writings of other political theorists. It was adopted by American conservatives anxious about totalitarianism in Europe as well as identity politics here in the United States. Hannah Arendt gives an updated Burkean analysis of how authenticity and identity politics can, in the extreme, lead to the death of substantive argument and thus politics altogether. As Margaret Canovan noted, Arendt's philosophy follows a long line of conservative thought from Burke to Oakeshott in that it sought to impose "a politics of limits" to counter the utopian imaginations of romantics and revolutionaries.[12] Arendt's Burkean analysis defends the costumes, roles, and institutional factors necessary to thwart the onslaught of violent, thoughtless mobocracy.

America challenged Burkean assumptions in the middle of the twentieth century with an explosion of identity politics. As mentioned in our
chapter on authenticity, feminists, civil rights advocates, and student radicals called not primarily for representatives and office-holders to change
policy, but for direct action by the very persons who were oppressed or
claimed to speak for the oppressed. They also fought for the right to
express themselves directly in public rather than being forced into social
roles. As Jay Magill writes, "[r]ebelling against the conformity of the
1940s and 1950s, hippies were Rousseau's dream come true: freedom to
be who you really are, a return to nature unadorned."[13] In many ways, this
repeated the same left-right debate over personal vs. institutional politics
as the one in the eighteenth century between Burke and his radical coun-
terparts. As America entered a period of unprecedented affluence and
democratization, many these new, "post-material" reform movements,
especially radical student movements, had less to do with physical emancipation from bondage than with creating spaces for expression of one's
identity. Students for a Democratic Society (SDS) produced the *Port
Huron Statement*, much of which closely reflected Rousseau's vision of
authentic individuality found in his *Discourses*. In it, they gave a statement
that guided the New Left in its social and political vision:

> Men have unrealized potential for self-cultivation, self-direction, self-
> understanding, and creativity. It is this potential that we regard as crucial
> and to which we appeal, not to the human potentiality for violence, unrea-
> son, and submission to authority. The goal of man and society should be
> human independence: a concern not with image of popularity but with find-
> ing a meaning in life that is personally authentic: a quality of mind not
> compulsively driven by a sense of powerlessness, nor one which unthink-
> ingly adopts status values, nor one which represses all threats to its habits,
> but one which has full, spontaneous access to present and past experiences,
> one which easily unites the fragmented parts of personal history, one which
> openly faces problems which are troubling and unresolved: one with an
> intuitive awareness of possibilities, an active sense of curiosity, an ability and
> willingness to learn.[14]

The SDS sought to achieve a society in which humans reach their full
potential without being hindered by institutional rules of the past, not be
judged by appearances. Feminists of the 1960s argued along similar lines,
as Betty Friedan sought to lift the traditional veil of being a housewife,

setting off a movement to bring women out of the home and into public life. Women, rather than playing a pre-assigned domestic role, began calling for their right to self-expression: "The only way for a woman, as for a man, to find herself, to know herself as a person, is by creative work of her own."[15] Martin Luther King, in perhaps his most widely quoted formulation, asked that his children not to be "judged by the color of their skin but by the content of their character." Oppressed groups ought to be able to express themselves in a transparent way to other citizens as equals, without the need to shroud themselves in traditional cloaks of womanhood, youth, sexuality, or identities attached to skin color or nationality.

Perhaps the most poignant instance of identity politics after the 1960s was the *Combahee River Collective Statement*. As lesbian, economically underprivileged women of color, the group wrote from several different perspectives of oppression. In their individual identities, they found a politicized group identity:

> We are a collective of Black feminists who have been meeting together since 1974. During that time we have been involved in the process of defining and clarifying our politics, while at the same time doing political work within our own group and in coalition with other progressive organizations and movements. The most general statement of our politics at the present time would be that we are actively committed to struggling against racial, sexual, heterosexual, and class oppression, and see as our particular task the development of integrated analysis and practice based upon the fact that the major systems of oppression are interlocking. The synthesis of these oppressions creates the conditions of our lives. As Black women we see Black feminism as the logical political movement to combat the manifold and simultaneous oppressions that all women of color face ... There is also undeniably a personal genesis for Black Feminism, that is, the political realization that comes from the seemingly personal experiences of individual Black women's lives.[16]

The statement demonstrates the inversion of Lockean, Burkean disembodied rationality, through which modern conservatives had always defined themselves. One's public views came to be defined by one's private life, particularly a private life in which oppression was the paramount experience. To do politics meant to engage in a Rousseauist/Marxist unveiling from a place of seclusion, and then a public exposition of what was unveiled.

The left's argument for this unveiling, conservatives argued, was often utopian, especially when expressed through identity politics or mass movements. Conservatives used a mixture of Lockean reasoning about the marketplace and Burkean caution about institutions to argue that that markets, and the government institutions that bolstered them, were free of emotion, and therefore superior to movements that made anger, grievance, and exclusion their moral foundations. And against what they saw as utopianists and identity groups on the left, they argued that individuals cannot shape the world themselves. Kim Phillips-Fein describes the rise of the conservative capitalism of Friedrich Hayek in *Invisible Hands*:

> Hayek saw himself working in the intellectual tradition of John Locke, Bernard Mandeville, and Adam Smith, but also that of Edmund Burke and Alexis de Tocqueville. Like Burke, the late eighteenth century philosopher of counterrevolution, he mistrusted the arrogance of rationalism, the idea that people could understand and shape the world; and like Tocqueville, he was suspicious of the will of the majority. But where Burke asked his readers to recall tradition, the endless, infinite wisdom of the ages embodied in every customary relationship, the Austrian thinkers looked to the marketplace. The ebb and flow of the market brought together all the bits of information in society, more innumerable and complex than any single human mind could ever hope to assimilate.[17]

Philosophically, conservatives stood firmly against the modern urge to remake the world in one's image, or to fight for immediate inclusion, but rather to find oneself in the midst of a complex world no one could or should try to control. William F. Buckley's remark that "conservatism implies a certain submission to reality" was meant to limit politics to the realm of the possible and to expel utopian visions, from Rousseau to the hippies of the 1960s, from political consideration. The conservatism of Hayek, Buckley, and then Barry Goldwater attempted to promote was based on two related rejections of the politics of authenticity; it believed that one ought to argue politics after detaching oneself personally from the issue and that American constitutional traditions always separated the "political" realm from the "social" realm. Barry Goldwater's opposition to civil rights legislation in the 1960s was based on his view of impersonal, constitutional law. In a speech given on this, Goldwater details how he was personally opposed to racial discrimination but that he did not see a legal solution for it. The problem with civil rights legislation is not, for

Goldwater, that the goal is wrong but that the haste to achieve it makes ruin of the deliberative character of the legislative body:

> I wish to make myself perfectly clear. The two portions of this bill to which I have constantly and consistently voiced objections, and which are of such overriding significance that they are determinative of my vote on the entire measure, are those which would embark the Federal government on a regulatory course of action with regard to private enterprise in the area of so-called 'public accommodations' and in the area of employment—to be more specific, Titles II and VII of the bill.
>
> I find no constitutional basis for the exercise of Federal regulatory authority in either of these two areas; and I believe the attempted usurpation of such power to be a grave threat to the very essence of our basic system of government, namely, that of a constitutional republic in which fifty sovereign states have reserved to themselves and to the people those powers not specifically granted to the central or Federal government.
>
> If it is the wish of the American people that the Federal government should be granted the power to regulate in these two areas and in the manner contemplated by this bill, then I say that the Constitution should be so amended by the people as to authorize such action in accordance with the procedures for amending the Constitution which that great document itself prescribes.
>
> I say further that for this great legislative body to ignore the Constitution and the fundamental concepts of our governmental system is to act in a manner which could ultimately destroy the freedom of all American citizens, including the freedoms of the very persons whose feelings and whose liberties are the major subject of this legislation.
>
> My basic objection to this measure is, therefore, constitutional.[18]

For Rousseau and those who believe in the politics of authenticity, Goldwater's statement is indicative of the inherent hypocrisy in a constitutional government: how could one personally be in favor of a measure that they constitutionally oppose? After all, laws are made by people. Yet this is why for conservatives since Burke, the idea of having dual identities, personal and political, is central to stability in political life; one does not automatically feel compelled to politicize their personal beliefs.

The midcentury political debate between left and right was largely over the extent to which "the personal" ought to be considered "political."

This debate extended into questions of intellectual life. The right argued for a detachment of oneself from academic or literary pursuits. The left increasingly demonstrated the idea that injecting the self into those pursuits made them into more meaningful and interesting undertakings. This is a rift that would last for several decades. The beats, led by Jack Kerouac and Allen Ginsberg, displayed a rebellious, free-form type of expression both in their literary style and in the lived experiences that it detailed. Ginsberg's *Howl* made several explicit sexual references, making an intensely private realm into a public one. Kerouac's *On the Road* similarly defied the norms by showing rebellious young drifters breaking out of their assigned social roles. While the beats saw themselves as free and original, conservative commentator Norman Podhoretz saw them as nothing more than unserious anti-intellectuals. In his essay "The Know Nothing Bohemians," Podhoretz laments that Kerouac is "thoroughly unpolitical" and that "he seems to feel that respectability is a sign … of spiritual death." Podhoretz contrasts earlier forms of literary rebellion with that of the 1950s, which he sees as virtually nihilistic:

> The Bohemianism of the 1950s … is hostile to civilization; it worships primitivism, instinct, energy, 'blood.' To the extent that it has intellectual interests at all, they run to mythical doctrines, irrationalist philosophies, and left-wing Reichianism. The only art the new Bohemians have any use for is jazz, mainly the cool variety. Their predilection for bop language is a way of demonstrating solidarity with the primitive vitality and spontaneity they find in jazz and of expressing contempt for coherent, rational discourse which, being a product of the mind, is in their view a form of death. To be articulate is to admit that you have no feelings ….[19]

To Podhoretz, the sheer expression of feelings and the unveiling of "primitive" human nature we see in Kerouac and Ginsberg were unpolitical, unrefined, and intellectually deadening, just as Rousseau's celebration of primitivism was to Burke. When this thoughtless and reactive tendency to inject one's self or identity into complex political matters spreads, conservatives warned, a politics of difference dies altogether and we are on the road back to totalitarianism. We see this fear in Allan Bloom's *Closing of the American Mind* in which he lamented that self-expressive Black Panthers and other "politically correct" identity groups had dangerously stifled intellectual pursuits. Bloom recalled a scene of "ten thousand" students threatening professors at Cornell University with violence and lamented that "[t]he American university in the sixties was experiencing the same dismantling of the structure of rational inquiry as had the German university in the thirties." Bloom went on to compare the New Left in America to the death of politics that led to Nazi Germany:

> In both [Germany and the United States] the universities gave way under the pressure of mass movements, and did so in large measure because they thought those movements possessed a moral truth superior to any the university could provide. Commitment was understood to be profounder than science, passion than reason, history than nature, and young than old. In fact, as I have argued, the thought was really the same. The New Left in America was a Nietzscheanized-Heideggerianized Left. The unthinking hatred of 'bourgeois society' was exactly the same in both places. A distinguished professor of political science proved this when he read to his radical students some speeches about what was to be done. They were enthusiastic until he informed them that the speeches were by Mussolini.[20]

In a twist of irony, Donald Trump, who led his old mass movement in 2015–2016, and became even more institutionalized as president than Bloom's derided college radicals, tweeted a quote from Mussolini, also without knowing who the author was.[21]

Just as Arendt believed Rousseau, the Jacobins, and totalitarian regimes dangerously attempted to perfect society by stifling the fluctuations of politics for the sake of moral purity, American conservatives charged the left with doing the same. Arendt lent her own voice to the conservative anxiety that the moral push for equality by identity groups tended to supplant formal, constitutional institutions with immediate, extraconstitutional solutions. This push, argued Arendt, often created the wrong solutions for the particular grievance or did nothing at all to address it. This was not to say that direct action is always wrong in itself. But when it was done simply to "let off steam" it became apolitical and fruitless.[22] Moreover, she explains, we often fall into the realm of the intangible and invisible once "letting off steam" becomes common practice. For instance, Arendt offered a controversial, reactionary critique of what today might be called "white guilt": "it has become rather fashionable among white liberals to react to Negro grievances with the cry, 'we are all guilty,' and Black Power has proved only too happy to take advantage of this 'confession' to instigate an irrational 'black rage'." This ritual, for Arendt, does nothing to address the problem and creates "a dangerous and obfuscating escalation of racism into some higher, less tangible regions."[23] Arendt castigates the left in this practice by connecting it back to the "war on hypocrisy" that was central to the Jacobins' rage during the French Revolution. The genesis of today's apolitical state, Arendt argues, began when the Jacobins decided that "[w]ords can be relied on only if one is sure that their function is to reveal and not to conceal." This leads to a never-ending, paranoid "hunt for suspects, accompanied by the psychological hunt for ulterior motives" behind individuals' public words. We end up, in other words, doing psychoanalysis rather than politics. Mid- to late-century conservatism thus called into question the Rousseauist merging of the personal with the political.

THE BACKLASH

Since the 1960s, American conservatism has cultivated its own brand of populist authenticity. It has adopted many of the same tenets of the politics of authenticity that conservatives had lamented about leftism in the past: the elevation of private expression over public discourse, the tearing off of social masks defined before and outside of the individual, the primacy of "truth" in politics rather than its fluctuations. The left in the 1960s created a political climate that thrived on personality and self-expression. The right took this mantle by the afterward.

Ronald Reagan's demeanor and appeal was that he was an authentic American who personified the best of American traditions: hard work and family values. By the 1990s, the "morning in America" optimism exuded by Reagan began to give way to a more adversarial right-wing populism that pitted average, authentic Americans against seemingly artificial elites in government, academia, and the media. Just as the beat and hippie generations had, the right was producing its own form of anti-elitist populism. Thomas Frank writes about what he calls the "backlash" of conservative Americans against the perceived excesses of leftist identity groups:

> In the backlash imagination, America is always in a state of quasi-civil war: on the one side are the unpretentious millions of authentic Americans; on the other stand the bookish, all-powerful liberals who run the country but are contemptuous of the tastes and beliefs of the people who inhabit it. When the chairman of the Republican National Committee in 1992 announced to a national TV audience, 'We are America' and 'those other people are not,' he was merely giving new and more blunt expression to a decades-old formula. Newt Gingrich's famous description of Democrats as 'the enemy of normal Americans' was just one more winning iteration of this well-worn theme.[24]

Podhoretz and Bloom had lamented the anti-intellectualism of the beats, hippies, and other identity groups advocating "personal expression." Those groups were anti-intellectual, conservatives believed, because they insisted on injecting the personal into the political, rather than understanding politics from an impersonal, objective standpoint. But now conservatism itself was becoming more personal; it was injecting an identity of "Americanism" into a grievance politics the same way the left had injected its own plethora of identities.

Many conservative elites have, as a matter of principle, still sought to maintain the idea that identity politics leads to unreasonable political demands. Paul Ryan, who during the Trump presidential campaign became a de facto leader of the Republican establishment, said, "I would argue that the left basically perfected identity politics. It's very effective, but it's very divisive, and we on the Right should not come anywhere close to it. I believe in inclusive, aspirational politics that speaks to our common humanity." Conservative Jonah Goldberg similarly derides Trump's appeal as essentially white nationalist, which is just as corrosive as the identity politics of the left:

> If nationalism is supposed to do anything, it's supposed to unify the country. When I look at these so-called nationalists, though, I don't see a unifying force. I see the latest entrants into a decades-old game of subdividing the country into tribes seeking to yoke government to their narrow agendas.[25]

The veneer that the Democratic Party is a coalition of identity groups and self-expressive, anti-establishment radicals and that the Republican Party is the sober counterpart focused on policy is difficult to keep up after the nomination and election of Donald Trump. There are three main features of right-wing populism that resulted in Donald Trump, that echo the Jacobins and co-opt elements of the politics of authenticity that had been mainstays of the left. One was the desire for plain-spoken, authentic office-seekers. The second was an identity politics about which leaders of the Republican Party could only speak in code, until Trump. The third was a conspiratorial mindset that not only painted institutions as inherently corrupt, but also charged all motives of "establishment" politicians within those institutions as having evil intentions.

Trump routinely spoke without a teleprompter. Like most people, when they are conversing at informal settings, Trump seemed to have no preparation for speeches he made. Since his rhetoric was often unprepared, it made it seem that Trump had no ulterior motives in his speeches other than to "tell the truth." In doing this, Trump would keep his words simple and short. Linguist Jennifer Sclafani says that

> [Trump's] unique rhetorical style may come off as incoherent and unintelligible when we compare it with the organized structure of other candidates' answers. On the other hand, his conventional style may also help construct an identity for him as authentic, relatable and trustworthy, which are qualities that voters look for in a presidential candidate.[26]

Trump used simple words throughout the campaign to make clear points and to relate to his audience. Sclafani goes on to describe how instead of using the Latin-derived words like "immigrate" and "deport" to describe his immigration policies, he uses shorter, Germanic verb phrases like "come in," "go out," and "come back" when discussing movements of immigrants in and out of the country. The lamentations of mid-twentieth-century conservatives like Podhoretz over the "primitivism" of the beats may have applied here as well.

This speaking style of Trump in many ways might have been the manifestation of Rousseau's vision of authenticity from 300 years ago. While Trump may have been ignorant of many political issues, the simplicity and straightforwardness of his language was indicative of a figure not corrupted by institutional norms. It mirrored Rousseau's idea that "the plain and noble effusions of an honest soul speak a language far different from the insincere demonstrations of politeness (and the false appearances) which the customs of the great world demand."[27] Trump and his supporters feel punished, Rousseau might offer, because "all kinds of frankness and honesty are terrible crimes in the eyes of society."[28]

Like the Jacobins or the left of the 1960s, Trump and his supporters routinely claimed that they were the victims of an unfair political, media, and cultural environment. Like Rousseau, the politeness and social customs and norms, as well as the institutions of formal politics, not only made people hypocrites, but it buried this injustice behind masks. The most important signifier of their victimhood was their whiteness. Since the late 1960s, when Kevin Phillips wrote *The Emerging Republican Majority*, as a guidebook to conservatives winning power on the basis of white resentment, conservatives had to speak in code in most parts of the country about white identity.[29] President Barack Obama attempted to assuage white grievance politics by equating it with the anger felt by African Americans:

> In fact, a similar anger exists within segments of the white community. Most working- and middle-class white Americans don't feel that they have been particularly privileged by their race. Their experience is the immigrant experience—as far as they're concerned, no one handed them anything. They built it from scratch. They've worked hard all their lives, many times only to see their jobs shipped overseas or their pensions dumped after a lifetime of labor. They are anxious about their futures, and they feel their dreams slipping away.[30]

Yet conservatives zeroed in on an audio recording just a month later, in which Obama suggested that cultural preferences of white, working class voters in failing post-industrial areas of the country were irrational: "They get bitter, they cling to guns or religion or antipathy to people who aren't like them or anti-immigrant sentiment or anti-trade sentiment as a way to explain their frustrations."[31] White voters themselves rarely said publicly that their whiteness was a source of oppression. But Trump came closer than any presidential candidate in modern history to explicitly saying that whites are being systematically discriminated against. This was exactly what a large segment of his supporters believed. In a poll from June 2016, 72% of Republicans said that they believed whites are discriminated against at least as much as minority groups. The percentage for Trump supporters was 81%.[32] The grievance politics of the right is due partly on the fact that social justice movements of the 1960s became institutionalized. In an interview with podcaster Ezra Klein, political scientist Lilliana Mason describes the role reversal on anti-establishment populism that the left and right have undergone since the 1960s:

> The fact that we have these racial and religion lines aligned with our partisan identities actually is a big threat to the traditional social hierarchy of our society. And that caused this mass freak-out. And ultimately, after Trump is done ... we will know this is our fight. The cleavage between our parties is a social justice cleavage. That's what it is. And it took [Trump's election] to get us to admit that that's what the new partisan cleavage is. And then our parties fight along that line. Our party divisions have always been moving. Sometimes we fight over economics, sometimes we fight over culture. But the line keeps moving ... So this might be like the 60s if we didn't have a party representing social justice right now. Part of what happened in the

> 60s is that the populists were fighting for social justice, and there was no organized place to put it. And it turned into absolute chaos. And right now … what we're doing is putting it an organized place in the Democratic Party.[33]

We can make the inference that since the anti-institutionalist left became institutionalized after the 1960s, the right grew increasingly *anti*-institutionalist.

Given the realignment of anti-institutionalist populism, it is no surprise that Trump supporters also believed that the country needed a leader who would "break some rules" at the rate of 72%.[34] Acting outside of formal political mechanisms is central to the tactics of the politics of authenticity. This is not only for the purpose of solving public problems but, more importantly, to break out of a claustrophobic culture that stifles freedom of self-expression. Radicals in the 1960s had demonstrated free love in the open rather than in private, liberating sexuality from the shadows. Women sought to shake off their roles primarily as mothers and housewives. And African Americans sought to assert their shared identity with the Civil Rights and Black Power Movements. Trump sought to liberate the anger white identity politics from the confines of political correctness. Polls showed that whites were ready for such an unleashing. A Pew poll found that Trump supporters were much more likely than other Americans to believe that Mexican immigrants were prone to crime.[35] They also thought that African Americans were also prone to crime and less intelligent than whites.[36] And for Republican-leaning voters who supported Trump for the Republican nomination, 54% believed that whites were suffering because of society's special treatment for blacks and Hispanics.[37]

The growth in feelings of white oppression has been confirmed by other studies. Arlie Russell Hochschild engaged in a five-year sociological study detailing the resentments of poor white conservatives, most of whom became Trump supporters when he started running. She described their grievances as stemming from their perception that minority and other groups that had traditionally been seen as disadvantaged—African Americans, women, immigrants, and the like—had become "line-cutters." White working class resentment was not that government was too powerful, but that it was helping everyone but them.[38] Hochschild, who is not a conservative, attempts to take an empathetic view of the white working poor. Some conservatives have taken the same lessons from white working class resentment, but been less forgiving. Avik Roy, a movement conservative and an intellectual policy wonk, believes that the Republican Party now has little right to govern since it is based in white nationalism rather than free market conservative principles, as he had always assumed it was: "Until the conservative movement can stand up and live by that principle, it will not have the moral authority to lead the country."[39]

These feelings of resentment against a seemingly dominant class have led to a rise in conspiracy theories within the conservative movement in recent years. This, too, shares much in common with the paranoia of the Jacobins as well as that among some of the more radical, fringe elements of the 1960s and 1970s like the Weathermen. To be sure, conspiratorial movements on the right had always existed, from anti-immigrant Protestants, who thought Catholics drank blood in mass, to father Coughlin, to the John Birch Society. But those voices, while not always challenged by mainstream conservatives, were not central to the conservative movement. This borrowed a discourse from the radical, anti-establishment wing of the left, which had always been skeptical of power and feared that elites in government and elsewhere were conspiring against their revolutions and reforms. While 57% of Americans believed in the final weeks of the 2016 campaign that the election would be accurate and fair, more than two thirds of Trump voters believed—as Trump had himself announced repeatedly—that the vote would be "rigged."[40] The penchant for conspiracy theory had been central to populist conservatism for years and had swelled during the Obama administration. In 2015, 54% of conservatives believed that Barack Obama was a Muslim.[41] Donald Trump himself rose to political prominence in 2011 with claims that President Barack Obama had not been born in the United States. In 2013, a poll showed that 58% of Republicans believed that global warming was a hoax.[42] By May of 2018, almost half of Trump's supporters believed that between three million and five million Americans had voted illegally in the 2016 election.[43] All common measurements of objective truth, it seems, have been eradicated with Trumpism.

WE'RE ALL ANTI-INSTITUTIONALISTS NOW

In a 2011 episode of *The Rush Limbaugh Show*, the prominent right-wing radio host came up with a theory that he called "the four corners of deceit":

> We really live, folks, in two worlds. There are two worlds. We live in two universes. One universe is a lie. One universe is an entire lie. Everything run,

dominated, and controlled by the left here and around the world is a lie. The other universe is where we are, and that's where reality reigns supreme and we deal with it. And seldom do these two universes ever overlap. The Four Corners of Deceit: Government, academia, science, and media. Those institutions are now corrupt and exist by virtue of deceit. That's how they promulgate themselves; it is how they prosper.[44]

In 1988, linguist and left-wing intellectual Noam Chomsky had made a similar claim about how our epistemological framework was controlled by the right wing, not the left:

Perhaps this is an obvious point, but the democratic postulate is that the media are independent and committed to discovering and reporting the truth, and that they do not merely reflect the world as powerful groups wish it to be perceived. Leaders of the media claim that their news choices rest on unbiased professional and objective criteria, and they have support for this contention in the intellectual community. If, however, the powerful are able to fix the premises of the discourse, to decide what the general populace is allowed to see, hear, and think about, and to 'manage' public opinion by regular propaganda campaigns, the standard view of how the system works is at serious odds with reality.[45]

While the latter analysis is backed by well-sourced academic research, Limbaugh's assertions signal that the American right has learned how to politicize occlusion and grievance in a way that is effective. It is no surprise that beyond simply seeing the media as untrustworthy (which most Americans do), 60% of Trump supporters, following the lead of Donald trump and Steve Bannon, now think it is the "enemy of the American people."[46]

This merging of personal grievance with political ideology has been growing in recent years. Attempts to redivide the personal from the political have always animated elite American conservatism. When it comes to rearranging social relations between different races, sexes, or economic classes, the dominant, pragmatic wing of the conservative movement has adhered itself to the notion that "government can't legislate morality" and so it should not try. From its beginnings, modern conservatism has claimed that it scorns expressive politics that merely "lets off steam," which is either fruitless or dangerous, and, instead, seeks to solve social problems through appropriate legal channels in a slow, orderly fashion. From Burke to Arendt and beyond, it has always claimed to defend politics against utopian visions and cults of personality that claim to be able to solve all social problems. Accusers often become hysterical and hypocritical them-selves. We have seen with Trumpism that the elite leadership of the Republican Party has been holding together a fragile ideological base that was always vulnerable to appeals to white identity politics, if the right mes-senger showed up. In recent decades, whether because of electoral consid-erations or ideological shifting among conservative thinkers, American conservatism has attached itself to the type of dangerous utopianism, "war on hypocrisy," and conspiracy theory-style radicalism that it had always accused the left of perpetuating.

The center-left coalition of the Democratic Party, meanwhile, in the face of a perceived paranoid style in conservatism, has positioned itself as a quasi-Burkean party of moderation, reasonableness, and accuracy in pol-icy prescriptions and in the tone of argument. At the 2006 White House Correspondent Dinner, Stephen Colbert, perhaps reformulating William F. Buckley's case that "conservatism implies a certain submission to real-ity," phrased a favorite saying of progressives that "reality has a well-known liberal bias."[47] Amid increasing climate change denial among conserva-tives, Al Gore published a booked called *The Assault on Reason* in 2007. Barack Obama, during his administration, would often repeat a conserva-tive case against his policies and respond to it by saying that his plan was not based on politics, but "math."[48]

The anti-establishment ethos of Trump's Republican Party has not come without its intra-party casualties. "Never Trump" conservative com-mentators like George Will, Bill Kristol, and David Frum have either left the party, or tried to reform it from within. Arizona's Jeff Flake gave a rebuke of Trump in May 2018 at a commencement address at Harvard Law School. In it, he asked the graduating students to reflect on the Burkean-liberal formulation that we live within artificial institutions, and that justice takes time:

> For just a moment, let us marvel at the miracle that is the rule of law. We have seldom been moved to pause for such an appreciation, as we have been too busy taking it for granted and assuming its inviolability—like gravity. But unlike Newton's Laws, the rule of law was neither innate nor inevitable. What goes up must come down is a piece of cake compared to curbing the impulses of man and asking free people to abide rules and norms that form a country, and foster civilization.
>
> It took centuries of war and sacrifice and social upheaval and more war and great civil rights struggles to establish the foundational notion that no one

is either above the law or unworthy of the protections afforded by a robust legal system, a system that took us from feudal servility to a constitutional model that is the envy of the world. And will continue to be, with your help.[49]

Jeff Flake's speech speaks to the justified fear of the loss of institutions, the theatrical decorum that is necessary for those institutions to function, and the unveiling of human nature that could lead to mob rule. Its framing, however obtuse to the struggles that oppressed Americans have faced over the centuries, is captured in the progressive maxim that "justice delayed is justice denied." There were many oppressed persons throughout American history that never got to live the successes that their movements eventually won, but who in their lifetimes rightfully sought to break through institutional barriers to their legal recognition.

Until Trump's election, establishment Republicans were unsure of how to speak to the base of its party, which, in retrospect, was clamoring for authentic, tell-it-like-it-is politics. Most have been mildly supportive of Trumpism while attempting not to answer to it much. Some were openly saying that identity politics is always dangerous no matter what ethnicity it represents. It does not look like the more populist, paranoid identity grievances that the elites in the party fear are going to disappear any time soon. The discourse of the politics of authenticity has been largely absent from academic literature since the 1960s, when "being yourself" was all the rage. As the conservative movement veers dangerously toward an apolitical authoritarianism, and private expression of grievance overtakes procedural politics, this discourse is needed more than ever.

Notes

1. *The Washington Post*, "Washington Post-ABC News national poll Sept. 5–8, 2016," http://apps.washingtonpost.com/g/page/politics/washington-post-abc-news-national-poll-sept-5-8-2016/2090/.
2. Alan Gomez, "Immigration Issue Largely Ignored; Trump Vows to Deport 'Bad Hombres'," *USA Today*, October 19, 2016, https://www.usatoday.com/story/news/2016/10/19/donald-trump-bad-hombres-hillary-clinton-presidential-debate/92442276/.
3. *MSNBC*, "MSNBC/Telemundo/Marist Poll, December 2015," http://msnbcmedia.msn.com/i/MSNBC/Sections/A_Politics/MSNBC_Telemundo_Marist%20Poll_National%20Annotated%20Questionnaire_December%202015.pdf.

4. Lazaro Gamio and Scott Clement, "South Carolina Republican Primary Exit Polls," *The Washington Post*, https://www.washingtonpost.com/graphics/politics/2016-election/primaries/south-carolina-exit-poll/.

5. Roger Scruton, *The Meaning of Conservatism* (South Bend, IN: St. Augustine's, 2002), 17.

6. Edmund Burke, *Reflections on the Revolution in France* (1790), accessed March 3, 2018, 64 https://socialsciences.mcmaster.ca/econ/ugcm/3ll3/burke/revfrance.pdf.

7. Peter Viereck, *Conservative Thinkers: From John Adams to Winston Churchill* (New Brunswick, NJ: Transaction, 2006), 118.

8. Burke, *Reflections*, 51–52.

9. Edmund Burke, *Further Reflections on the French Revolution* (1791), accessed March 3, 2018, http://oll.libertyfund.org/titles/burke-further-reflections-on-the-french-revolution.

10. Alexis de Tocqueville, *Democracy In America* (1836), accessed March 3, 2018, http://oll.libertyfund.org/titles/tocqueville-democracy-in-america-historical-critical-edition-vol-2.

11. John C Calhoun, *Slavery A Positive Good* (1837), accessed March 3, 2018, http://teachingamericanhistory.org/library/document/slavery-a-positive-good/.

12. see Margaret Canovan, *Hannah Arendt: A Reinterpretation of Her Political Thought* (Cambridge England: Cambridge University Press, 1992), 170.

13. Jay Magill, *Sincerity: How a Moral Ideal Born Five Hundred Years Ago Inspired Religious Wars, Modern Art, Hipster Chic, and the Curious Notion That We All Have Something to Say (no Matter How Dull)* (New York: Norton, 2012), 168.

14. Students for a Democratic Society "The Port Huron Statement" in *American Political Thought*, ed. Kenneth M. Dolbeare (Chatham, NJ: Chatham House, 1998), 492–93.

15. Betty Friedan, *The Feminine Mystique* (New York: W.W. Norton, 1963), 472.

16. The Combahee River Collective, "The Combahee River Collective Statement, accessed March 20, 2018, https://americanstudies.yale.edu/sites/default/files/files/Keyword%20Coalition_Readings.pdf.

17. Kim Phillips-Fein, *Invisible Hands: the Making of the Conservative Movement from the New Deal to Reagan* (New York: Norton, 2009), 37.

18. Barry Goldwater, "When Unconstitutional Laws Are Passed" (1964), accessed March 8, 2018, http://www.citizenreviewonline.org/jan_2003/when.htm.

19. Norman Podhoretz, "The Know Nothing Bohemians," in *The New York Intellectuals Reader*, ed. Neil Jumonville (Taylor and Francis, 2013), 309.

20. Allan Bloom, *The Closing of the American Mind* (New York: Simon and Schuster, 1987), 314–15.
21. Maggie Haberman, "Donald Trump Retweets Post With Quote From Mussolini," *The New York Times*, February 16, 2016, https://www.nytimes.com/politics/first-draft/2016/02/28/donald-trump-retweets-post-likening-him-to-mussolini/.
22. Hannah Arendt, *On Violence* (Harcourt, Brace and World, 1970), 63.
23. Arendt, *On Violence*, 63.
24. Thomas Frank, *What's the Matter with Kansas?: How Conservatives Won the Heart of America* (Metropolitan/Owl Books, 2005), 13.
25. Jonah Goldberg, "'New Nationalism' Amounts to Generic White-Identity Politics," *National Review*, August 17, 2016, https://www.nationalreview.com/2016/08/trumps-nationalism-white-identity-politics-brand-name/.
26. Stephanie Pappas, "Trump's Broken Speech Appeals to the Masses," *Live Science*, March 14, 2016, https://www.livescience.com/54035-donald-trump-broken-speech-appeals-to-masses.html.
27. Richard Sennett, *The Fall of Public Man* (Knopf, 1977), 118. Quoting Rousseau in *Julie.*
28. Jean-Jacques Rousseau, *Reveries of the Solitary Walker*, trans. Peter France (Penguin Books, 2004), 31.
29. see Phillips, Kevin Phillips, *The Emerging Republican Majority* (Princeton University Press, 2015).
30. Barack Obama, "A More Perfect Union," *The New York Times*, March 18, 2008, https://www.nytimes.com/2008/03/18/us/politics/18text-obama.html.
31. "Obama angers midwest voters with guns and religion remark," *The Guardian*, April 14, 2008, https://www.theguardian.com/world/2008/apr/14/barackobama.uselections2008.
32. "On Views of Race and Inequality, Blacks and Whites Are Worlds Apart," *Pew Research Center*, June 27, 2016, http://www.pewsocialtrends.org/2016/06/27/on-views-of-race-and-inequality-blacks-and-whites-are-worlds-apart/.
33. "The age of 'mega-identity' politics," interview of Lilliana Mason by Ezra Klein, *The Ezra Klein Show*, 4/30/2018, Audio 57:35, https://art19.com/shows/the-ezra-klein-show/episodes/11453d43-cd9e-4cf6-854f-f745261ad25a.
34. Aaron Blake, 'What Defines Trump Supporters? Take Republicans and make them wary of outsiders," *The Washington Post*, June 23, 2016, https://www.washingtonpost.com/news/the-fix/wp/2016/06/23/who-supports-donald-trump-take-a-republican-and-make-them-more-wary-of-outsiders/.

35. "On Immigration Policy, Partisan Differences but Also Some Common Ground," *Pew Research Center*, August 25, 2016, http://www.people-press.org/2016/08/25/on-immigration-policy-partisan-differences-but-also-some-common-ground/.
36. Emily Flitter and Chris Kahn, "Exclusive: Trump supporters more likely to view blacks negatively—Reuters/Ipsos poll," *Reuters*, June 28, 2016, http://www.reuters.com/article/us-usa-election-race-idUSKCN0Z-E2SW.
37. Scott Clement, "Discrimination against whites was a core concern of Trump's base," *The Washington Post*, August 2, 2017, https://www.washingtonpost.com/news/the-fix/wp/2017/08/02/discrimination-against-whites-was-a-core-concern-of-trumps-base/?utm_term=.2d14dacdb944.
38. Jason DeParle, "Why Do People Who Need Help From the Government Hate It So Much?," *The New York Times*, September 19, 2016, http://www.nytimes.com/2016/09/25/books/review/strangers-in-their-own-land-arlie-russell-hochschild.html?_r=0.
39. Zack Beauchamp, "A Republican intellectual explains why the Republican Party is going to die, "*Vox*, Jul 25, 2016, https://www.vox.com/2016/7/25/12256510/republican-party-trump-avik-roy. Quote from Avik Roy.
40. Susan Page and Karina Shedrofsky, "Poll: Clinton builds lead in divided nation worried about Election Day violence," *USA Today*, October 26, 2016, http://www.usatoday.com/story/news/politics/elections/2016/10/26/poll-clinton-builds-leads-nation-worried-election-day-violence-trump/92712708/.
41. Jesse Byrnes, "Poll: Majority of Republicans think Obama is a Muslim," *The Hill*, September 1, 2015, http://thehill.com/blogs/blog-briefing-room/news/252393-poll-majority-of-republicans-thinks-obama-is-a-muslim.
42. RP Siegel, "Poll: 58% of Republicans Still Believe Global Warming is a Hoax," *Triple Pundit*, Apr 25, 2013, https://www.triplepundit.com/2013/04/poll-58-republicans-believe-gloabal-warming-hoax/.
43. "HuffPost Voter Fraud Poll," *HuffPost*, May 17–20, 2018, https://big.assets.huffingtonpost.com/athena/files/2018/05/25/5b084adbe4b05 68a880b4571.pdf.
44. Heather Horn, "Is the Right Wing Anti-Science?," *The Atlantic*, September 10, 2010, https://www.theatlantic.com/politics/archive/2010/09/is-the-right-wing-anti-science/344226/.
45. Edward S. Herman and Noam Chomsky, *Manufacturing Consent: the Political Economy of the Mass Media* (Pantheon Books, 2002), ix.

46. Craig Silverman, "Trump is causing Democrats to trust media more, while Republicans are endorsing more extreme views, says a new study," *Poynter*, December 4, 2017, https://www.poynter.org/news/trump-causing-democrats-trust-media-more-while-republicans-are-endorsing-more-extreme-views.

47. Judd Legum, "Reality has a well-known liberal bias," *Think Progress*, April 30, 2006, https://thinkprogress.org/reality-has-a-well-known-liberal-bias-1f31539942c3#.xqjn10wf0.

48. Stephanie Condon, "Obama: 'This is not class warfare—It's math,'" *CBS News*, September 19, 2011, http://www.cbsnews.com/news/obama-this-is-not-class-warfare-its-math/.

49. Katie Reilly, "Read Jeff Flake's Commencement Speech on the Rule of Law and Trump: 'We May Have Hit Bottom'," *Time*, May 23, 2018, http://time.com/5289380/jeff-flake-harvard-commencement-address-president-trump/.

CHAPTER 7

Conclusion: Our Crisis of Authenticity

In *The Origins of Totalitarianism*, Hannah Arendt describes the attack on truth that takes place in totalitarian regimes:

> In an ever-changing, incomprehensible world the masses had reached the point where they would, at the same time, believe everything and nothing, think that everything was possible and that nothing was true .... Mass propaganda discovered that its audience was ready at all times to believe the worst, no matter how absurd, and did not particularly object to being deceived because it held every statement to be a lie anyhow. The totalitarian mass leaders based their propaganda on the correct psychological assumption that, under such conditions, one could make people believe the most fantastic statements one day, and trust that if the next day they were given irrefutable proof of their falsehood, they would take refuge in cynicism; instead of deserting the leaders who had lied to them, they would protest that they had known all along that the statement was a lie and would admire the leaders for their superior tactical cleverness.[1]

In a Fox News interview released June 22, 2017, Donald Trump was asked by Ainsley Earhardt about his false statement that he had taped conversation with FBI director James Comey:

AINSLEY EARHARDT (CO-HOST): Big news today. You said you didn't tape [former FBI Director] James Comey. Do you want to explain that? Why

155

D. J. McCool, *Three Frames of Modern Politics*,
https://doi.org/10.1007/978-3-319-95648-0_7

PRESIDENT DONALD TRUMP:

EARHARDT:

did you want him to believe you possibly did that?

Well I didn't tape him. You never know what's happening when you see that the Obama administration, and perhaps longer than that, was doing all of this unmasking and surveillance. And you read all about it and I've been reading about it for the last couple of months about the seriousness and horrible situation with surveillance all over the place. And you've been hearing the word "unmasking," a word you probably never heard before. So you never know what's out there, but I didn't tape and I don't have any tape and I didn't tape. But, when he found out that there may be tapes out there, whether it's governmental tapes or anything else, and who knows, I think his story may have changed. I mean, you'll have to take a look at that because then he has to tell what actually took place at the events. And my story didn't change. My story was always a straight story. My story was always the truth. But you'll have to determine for yourself whether or not his story changed. But, I did not tape.

That was a smart way to make sure he stayed honest in those hearings.[2]

Trump's deceitfulness was far from the only time tactical cleverness—facilitated by a foundation of public cynicism that "everybody lies"—was employed by Trump or his campaign. Right after Trump's inauguration, Kellyanne Conway told Chuck Todd of *Meet the Press* that the press secretary Sean Spicer had used "alternative facts" to assert that Trump's inauguration crowd was the largest in history.[3] Anyone who saw the pictures of the crowd size, then reflected on the facts that Donald Trump received a paltry share of the popular vote, had the lowest approval rating on Inauguration Day of any president in recent history, and had a penchant for conspiracy theories, knew that "alternative facts" was just another way of asserting one's right to propagandize.[4]

Observable facts did not matter in the closing days of the 2016 presidential election either. After Fox News host Bret Baier speculated on November 4, 2016, that the FBI's investigation into Hillary Clinton would "likely" end in indictment, he retracted it the next day: "It was a mistake and for that I'm sorry." The FBI itself then redacted its public statement that Clinton was under investigation. But by then, the story had already become ingrained into the closing campaign arguments of right-wing commentators. Rather than arguing that the retraction did not exonerate Clinton, pivoting to another issue with which to attack Clinton, or grudgingly acknowledging that the issue was no longer pertinent, Kellyanne Conway remarked to Brian Williams on MSNBC that "The damage is done to Hillary Clinton."[5]

This was astonishing. Conway and the Trump campaign had long ago decided that tactics, strategy, and perception were more important than observable truth. This has always been true in politics, but it is rarely admitted by campaigns. Trumpism had already established itself as a politics that almost self-consciously, and half-sardonically, exited the ritualistic performances by which voters, candidates, and the media abide. In this game, politicians and their campaigns act authentically outraged, and concerned for the country when their opponents do something that damages the public good or the public trust, and they pretend that public perception does not matter, but only what is right. Here, Clinton's offense had been exonerated, yet since the "damage [was] done," it was not worth pretending that the issue of a private email server was ever grounds for the Trump campaign's outrage in the first place. What mattered was public perception. It was not the job of the campaign to adhere to the truth, or to hold up the veneer that Clinton's conduct was not merely fodder for campaign attacks, but actually detrimental to the public good.

The campaign was now openly admitting that. The campaign itself had become the punditry. It is no wonder why the facts of the legal proceedings into the Trump campaign's misdeeds in 2016 are completely open to interpretation, depending on the tribe, and the cable news preferences, of the beholder.

We are facing the same type of obsession with privatist authenticity that Arendt described in the ascent of Jacobinism and totalitarianism. The rise of Trumpism is more than just a candidate simply saying what he thinks, or using theatrical flair to bring public attention to an issue. It is a noxious combination of the most authoritarian aspects of the politics of authenticity, mixed with the most truth-evasive aspects of the politics of theatricality, all while actively urging the delegitimization (rather than the improvement) of deliberative institutions. Like the Jacobins during the French Revolution, these tribal instincts take politics out of the realm of the visible, the tangible, and the concrete, and place them in the invisible realm of intention and innuendo. As we noted in the last chapter, Trump's voters appreciated his "tell-it-like-it-is" style above all else. What Trump "tells," however, are not observable, verifiable facts. He had told 3001 false or misleading claims in the eighteen months after his inauguration.[6] Rather, like the Jacobins, he tells of the nefarious intentions hiding behind all phony public appearances. What "is" is the suspicions we feel toward threatening people at any time, not their actions. This is why Barack Obama's birth certificate was a "phony." This is why the investigation against him was a "witch hunt," even after producing numerous indictments and guilty pleas.

Under populist authoritarianism, the suspicion of opponents' intentions and the theatrical shock value that ignites tribal instincts and public attention work in tandem in a war against perceived elites. In January 2017, the month of the inauguration of President Donald Trump, the Economist Intelligence Unit's (EIU) annual Democracy Index downgraded the United States from a "full democracy" to a "flawed democracy." While the downgrade was not a direct consequence of Donald Trump's election, his election was a symptom of larger problems.[7] Just before this report came out, the EIU released a report called "Revenge of the Deplorables." The authors investigate the reasons why 2016 witnessed a rebuke to the liberal democratic ideals. The authors explain:

The parallels between the June 2016 Brexit vote and the outcome of the November 8th US election are manifold. In both cases, the electorate defied the political establishment. Both votes represented a rebellion from below against out-of-touch elites. Both were the culmination of a long-term trend of declining popular trust in government institutions, political parties and politicians. They showed that society's marginalized and forgotten voters, often working-class and blue-collar, do not share the same values as the dominant political elite and are demanding a voice of their own—and if the mainstream parties will not provide it, they will look elsewhere. This is the main lesson for political leaders facing election in Europe in 2017 and beyond.[8]

This war against elites cannot be fought without widespread mistrust and near delegitimization of deliberative institutions, which is reaching crisis levels. The authors demonstrate that Americans' trust in government has plummeted since the 1950s. As of June 2016, less than one in five Americans "trust the government to do what is right" all or most of the time. Only 9% of respondents reported having any confidence at all in Congress. Not surprisingly, the authors say, populists are mobilizing these large sections of disaffected voters:

> The populists are channelling disaffection from sections of society that have lost faith in the mainstream parties. They are filling a vacuum and mobiliz- ing people on the basis of a populist, anti-elite message and are also appeal- ing to people's hankering to be heard, to be represented, to have their views taken seriously. Populist parties and politicians are often not especially coherent and often do not have convincing answers to the problems they purport to address, but they nevertheless post a challenge to the political mainstream because they are connecting with people who believe the estab- lished parties no longer speak for them.

This was hardly the first study detailing America's declining trust in political institutions. Robert Putnam's *Bowling Alone* warned of a fifty-year decline in America's social capital, which indicated both a decline in interpersonal trust and trust in institutions. Yousha Monk paints a dark picture of this populist moment in American and Western history:

> Citizens have long been disillusioned with politics; now, they have grown restless, angry, even disdainful. Party systems have long seemed frozen; now, authoritarian populists are on the rise around the world, from America to

Europe, and from Asia to Australia. Voters have long disliked particular parties, politicians, or governments; now, many of them have become fed up with liberal democracy itself.[9]

Andrew Sullivan writes before the election of Donald Trump, from a Burkean perspective, about how dangerous a position the United States is in right now, because of our severe lack of trust in elites and experts:

> As the authority of elites fades, as Establishment values cede to popular ones, views and identities can become so magnificently diverse as to be mutually uncomprehending. And when all the barriers to equality, formal and informal, have been removed; when everyone is equal; when elites are despised and full license is established to do "whatever one wants," you arrive at what might be called late-stage democracy. There is no kowtowing to authority here, let alone to political experience or expertise.

> Could it be that the Donald has emerged from the populist circuses of pro wrestling and New York City tabloids, via reality television and Twitter, to prove not just Plato but also James Madison right, that democracies 'have ever been spectacles of turbulence and contention … and have in general been as short in their lives as they have been violent in their deaths'? Is he testing democracy's singular weakness—its susceptibility to the demagogue—by blasting through the firewalls we once had in place to prevent such a person from seizing power? Or am I overreacting?

> Perhaps. The nausea comes and goes, and there have been days when the news algorithm has actually reassured me that 'peak Trump' has arrived. But it hasn't gone away, and neither has Trump. In the wake of his most recent primary triumphs, at a time when he is perilously close to winning enough delegates to grab the Republican nomination outright, I think we must confront this dread and be clear about what this election has already revealed about the fragility of our way of life and the threat late-stage democracy is beginning to pose to itself.[10]

Americans and other liberals around the world have always had a healthy skepticism toward governmental power and elite domination of politics. But this level of malaise is becoming increasingly destructive of our ability to confront public problems at all. This is not just psychological, but also material; Americans' growing distrust in institutions is not irrational when we consider the ways in which those institutions currently operate. Gilens and Page used multivariate analysis to find that in the 1980s and 1990s, economic elites completely dominated policy outcomes in American politics. They note:

> [o]ur analyses suggest that majorities of the American public actually have little influence over the policies our government adopts. Americans do enjoy many features central to democratic governance, such as regular elections, freedom of speech and association, and a widespread (if still contested) franchise. But we believe that if policy making is dominated by powerful business organizations and a small number of affluent Americans, than America's claims to being a democratic society are seriously threatened.[11]

In recent decades, Americans and citizens of other Western democracies have stopped believing that long-standing liberal institutions are responsive to the public. The very *perception* of government as a "swamp" or corrupt elites among American populists has created fertile ground for populist, radical, and reactionary political movements and leaders. While good-faith efforts to make democratic institutions more accountable to the needs of all racial, economic, and social classes in the public ought to be encouraged, attempts to delegitimize these institutions for the sake of settling grudges ought to be discouraged and openly fought. What makes today's anti-institutionalism so dangerous is that unlike in the 1960s, the new anti-institutionalists start off their fight *already* holding power. In fact, political science has shown that racial and ethnic tension, rather than economic anxiety, was responsible for Trump's base of support.[12] In a podcast interview with Ezra Klein, political scientist Yascha Mounk explains:

> The people who were aggrieved in the 50s and 60s were people who didn't have a ton of political power, which was deeply unjust, but also limited their ability to blow up the system. Now the people who are aggrieved—middle class, white men—have a *ton* of political power, and that makes it much easier for them to blow up the system.[13]

If these systems devolve further, Mounk explains: "I'm very, very worried that we have so little consensus now about how political institutions are supposed to work; what the limits are on what the president can do ... and that's predominantly on the right, but also on parts of the left ... I'm really scared that we'll devolve into dictatorial rule."[14] He goes on to warn:

> If we have a political system that allows a political entrepreneur to split us into these deeply tribal groups, and then to exploit that split into an attack

on the rules we need to live with each other, that's really dangerous. And let me put it this way: if you have deep disagreements, but you agree to a set of rules by which those disagreements can be managed and remedied, you're probably going to survive as a society. If you say 'I deeply disagree with you, I think you are wicked, but I am committed to a certain process by which we figure those disagreements out,' that may be unjust, because that may entail not challenging *slavery* enough. I'm not saying that American politics was *better* then, but it does mean that it is more likely to be stable.[15]

Echoing Lincoln's call for civil religion, Mounk calls on us not to try to rewrite the rules if the opposing party wins. Yet with the election of Donald Trump, anti-institutionalism *has* been institutionalized in the office of the presidency. It might take a generation or more to reestablish the primacy of institutional rule that Madison and Lincoln both cherished.

AUTHENTICITY IN AMERICAN POLITICS

Donald Trump's candidacy and presidency are a product of a larger era of politics in the modern world. As we have noted, speaking in a tell-it-like-it-is style has been beneficial for anti-institutionalist movements in the past. Throughout this book, we have been exploring the ways in which authenticity and theatricality have been theorized and exercised in modern politics since the Enlightenment. The norm of authenticity, it holds, dictates that one always tell the truth about oneself, that one maintain that voice of truth consistently across different audiences, and that, ideally, truth-telling can generate emancipatory politics for those persons who feel shut out of the free public sphere. This conception of authenticity seeks consistency and transparency between one's intentions and actions; between one's beliefs in past, present, and future beliefs; and finally between the unitary authentic self and others in the community. And perhaps most importantly for our political culture, "what is called politics" (as Henry David Thoreau reformulates it in *Civil Disobedience*) no longer centers on the shared, external realm of appearance as it did for the Greeks and even for the American founders, but on the dark recesses of the individual mind and soul: the conscience, the intention, and the morality of the individual.

For modern culture, authenticity remains the principal personal trait consumers of politics and culture look for in public figures. Yet the revolutionary edge of "being yourself" has given way to a consumer culture in which authenticity has been long been normalized (and, relatedly, commoditized). We can see this through many examples in the realms of politics and of pop culture in general. The American media (and its consumers, presumably) are shocked not necessarily when it discovers a nefarious act by an individual, but when it discovers that such an act creates a rift in an individual's private life and public presentation. Often, the private-public rift carries with it a more severe public castigation than the act itself. From Richard Nixon to Bill Cosby, the uncovering of the veneer of the public mask is seen by itself as a political act. Donald Trump has saved us the suspense of uncovering the public persona, by acting in public exactly how people think he acts in private. We are numb to the dark personal secrets that would have led to dequalification for office, or even for any public esteem, had it been any other figure without his marketing skills.

All this is not to say that hidden intentions, the rift between private and public selves, and the sincerity of public actors ought not to ever be highlighted at all in our public discourse. We ought to be able to occasionally judge private intentions in public life. For instance, the difference in the severity of the punishment for first-degree and second-degree murder is valid since one is based on more nefarious inner intentions behind the act. Likewise, judging the perceived intentions of public officials is inescapable. It is when intention is the overwhelming or only concern that we lose sight of the idea that political outcomes are collective endeavors, guided by circumstances and institutions, not simply the result of an individual's inner intentions. For the last two presidents, public judgment of their characters dominated their opposing tribes while they were in office. In the 2000s, liberals bemoaned the idea that George W Bush was unabashed about making decisions based on his "gut" rather than on what they saw as nuanced facts and evidence in the real world. In *The New York Times*, Ron Suskind suggests that Bush's own focus on his inner self in interviews about public policy stems from his born-again experience, a quite personal, inner-directed way of transforming one's self in the world.[16] This is not dissimilar from the Protestant theories of Luther and the quasi-Protestant writings of Rousseau, who, as noted earlier, both stress the centrality of the inner life, both in political action and in judgment of political action. The effects that the Iraq War had on America's international concerns seemed secondary. Conservatives also focused their judgment on the inner intentions of Barack Obama. David Limbaugh, author of *The Great Destroyer: Barack Obama's War on the Republic*, asks a number of rhetorical questions:

> Does Obama harbor a grudge against America? What did he mean when he said he wanted to fundamentally change America? What did his wife mean when she said she'd never been proud of America in her adult life before he rose to power? What possesses Obama to deride and apologize for America?

Limbaugh's answer is that while he does not believe Barack Obama is intentionally trying to "destroy America" (which, he grants, is a perfectly valid question), he does not assign good intentions behind Obama's actions, since "Obama, like so many leftist radicals, has a strong distaste for pre-Obama America."[17] While Bush seemed to encourage an intense public focus on his intentions more than Obama, for both, we ought not fall completely into the darkness of their inner selves. To the degree that we pretend to know the hidden "self" of each behind the mask, we create a politics that ignores the world their policies are creating. This contemporary practice has a recent history based on the cultural, technological, and media contexts of the twentieth and twenty-first centuries. On many fronts, American politics today has been stripped of its public character and has focused on the inner private self to the detriment of politics. As a result, we are living in a claustrophobic sea of Trumpism, where the power of the president's character traits dominates our discourse. This has set a dangerous stage for a cult of personality that transcends all concerns over specific policies, or an anti-institutionalist, glacial sliding toward authoritarianism.

AUTHENTICITY AND "THE CENTURY OF THE SELF"

Trump's cult of personality had its roots in the 1960s. The hopeful ideal of the sovereign, authentic self began with Rousseau and was destroyed by twentieth-century mass society and totalitarianism, under the weight of its own logic. Similarly, authenticity was introduced into the culture as a liberating force in the 1960s, only to be used as a conformist marketing tool by the end of the century. Like other social and political movements that have been discussed in this book, the hippie movement of the 1960s saw the ideal of authenticity as a bedrock, yet the ideal became monopolized and utilized by the same forces it perceived as oppressive. This rise and demise of authenticity from the 1960s onward is captured in the BBC documentary *The Century of the Self*.[18] The film details the high ideals of the New Left as it sought to fight the effects of perceived state oppression. Faced with the overwhelming power of the state, the narrator argues, "many in the New Left began to turn to a new idea: if it was impossible to get the policeman out of one's head by overthrowing the state, instead one should find a way of getting inside one's own mind and removing the controls implanted there by the state and the corporations. Out of this would come a new self and thus, a new society."[19] A collectivity of newly authentic selves would, in the aggregate, create a more authentic society. This new idea became the foundation, the film argues, of the Human Potential Movement (HPM), which was founded by psychotherapists who created the Esalen Institute in Big Sur, California. In group therapy meetings, individuals were encouraged, as Rousseau encouraged child-rearers to treat their children in *Emile* two centuries before, to express natural emotions that had been discouraged and suppressed in regular society. Expressing their "true inner selves" was a means toward self-recovery, creating "new autonomous beings, free of social conditioning."[20] One can see and trace these radical virtues to the reactionary outbursts of anti-politically correct slogans shouted at Trump's 2016 rallies. In both cases, the institutional and social veils covering our naked human nature had been lifted.

By the late 1960s, this ideal of autonomy and authenticity had spread. This began to concern corporate America, since "these new selves were not behaving as predictable consumers." This changed the ways in which corporations began to sell products to Americans. As the narrator of *The Century of the Self* notes, new costumers "no longer wanted anything that would place them within the narrow strata of American society. Instead what they wanted were products that would express their individuality, their difference in a conformist world." Market researcher Daniel Yankelovich details in the film that "products have always had an emotional meaning. What was new was individuality; the idea that 'this product expresses me'." This logic then applied to cars, music, and clothes. "Operating groups" were set up within corporations to try to discern how to appeal to new consumers seeking individual authenticity. One agency head wrote to his operating group: "We must conform to the new nonconformists. We must listen to the music of Bobby Dylan and go to the theatre more."

Not only did corporate America began devising ways to reach these new consumers, but the consumers themselves were beginning to shed the political idealism that initially inspired this updated politics of authenticity, focusing instead on remaking themselves rather than the world, Rousseau's radical individuality without the collectivist ideals. The film details new self-help movements, seminars, and ideas that began to emerge that attempted to strip away socially implanted conformist tendencies. But unlike the HPM these new movements did so not to discover a core inner *goodness* of the self; that idea itself was too constricting. Instead, they sought to strip away every layer of the self until what was revealed inside was an ethically neutral blank slate of nothingness and meaninglessness. From here, one could rebuild oneself and one's reality in the world in an even more authentic, voluntary way. As the film describes it, "one of the original Yippie founders Jerry Rubin ... was beginning to buy into the notion that he could be happy and fully self-developed on his own: socialism in one person ... which of course is capitalism!" Having dropped the "inner goodness" side of the formula advocated by the Esalen Institute, self-help movements began to drop the "political" aspirations of the "personal is political" formulation that influenced so many political activists of the 1960s. The Rousseauist project of rediscovering moral virtue in the heart of the natural individual, and then turning that individual virtue into collective justice, had lost out to the licentiousness of the 1970s, 1980s, and beyond in which the mere product preferences of the ethically neutral self became paramount. In this atmosphere, corporations, which the hippie movement originally saw as the colonizers of the authentic self, had no problems creating and then fulfilling the desires of a more libertine consumer market. Like past attempts to create a more authentic society in which the self was equipped to resist manipulation, the movements of the 1960s simply created new avenues through which public manipulation could be exercised.

These new forms of corporate domination influenced the political world as well. The film goes on to detail the ways in which politicians in the 1980s and 1990s harnessed this new nexus of authenticity and corporate influence to win elections and public favor. Consumer research firms like Stanford Research Institute came up with new ways to categorize people, not based on traditional categories like race, age, or class, but by lifestyles that people adopted in order to express themselves. This new style of categorization became infused with political campaigns. Particularly, Ronald Reagan's 1980 campaign tapped into this new style of individuality by focusing not on governmental problem-solving, but the new individualistic value of *choice*, a byproduct of the self-help movements of the

1960s and 1970s. Reagan and Margaret Thatcher, the film argues, appealed to the "inner-directed" individuals that research firms had identi- fied. According to Christine MacNulty, Program Manager of The SRI Values and Lifestyles Team from 1978 to 1981, new consumers

> were really concerned about being individuals, being individualistic. And so in the early stages [of the Reagan and Thatcher campaigns] when we were looking at the messages both Thatcher and Reagan were putting across, we said 'they are using words that will really appeal to a lot of the younger people, and particularly to the people who are moving toward self- actualization.' We call them the "inner-directed" people. A lot of our col- leagues said 'that's absolutely ridiculous, because inner-directeds are very socially-aware ... they'll never vote conservative.' But we said 'if Thatcher and Reagan continue to appeal to them in this way, they really will.'"

Thus, the new marketing power of authenticity, ironically, came to be increasingly employed by the right in efforts to undo or slow down many of the social gains of the 1960s and 1970s.

THE DECLINE OF PUBLIC TRUST

At the same time that Americans began focusing more on remaking them- selves than remaking the world, the American media began the decades- long endeavor of covering personal scandal in politics. Just as corporate America and its consumers turned "personal," so too did our judgments of political events and, with it, our assessments of the "characters" of office-holders and candidates. While personality had always played a role in the assessment of public actors throughout American history, coverage of Richard Nixon's personality greatly damaged trust in governmental fig- ures for at least a generation. Historian Julian Zelizer argued in 2004 that "[w]e still live in the era of Watergate." Zelizer argues:

> The worst effect of Watergate is that it created a climate where Americans fundamentally don't trust their government. It is one thing to be suspicious, another to reject government altogether. Recent approval ratings for Congress tanked to 7% and for the President, 29%. This is part of the broader trend we have seen since the 1960s. It is extremely difficult for government to do its job or for voters to have the kind of faith in govern- ment, which is necessary for a healthy society.[21]

Filmmakers Ken Burns and Lynn Novick point out how the events of the Vietnam War specifically eroded trust in the office of the presidency ever since:

> It did not happen all at once, this radical diminution of trust. Over more than a decade, the accumulated weight of critical reporting about the war, the publication of the Pentagon Papers in 1971, and the declassification of military and intelligence reports tarnished the office. Nor did the process stop when that last chopper took off. New evidence of hypocrisy has contin-ued to appear, an acidic drip, drip, drip on the image of the presidency. The three men who are most responsible for the war, John F. Kennedy, Lyndon B. Johnson, and Richard Nixon, each made the fateful decision to record their deliberations about it. The tapes they left behind—some of them still newly public, others long obscured by the sheer volume of the material—are extraordinary. They expose the presidents' secret motives and fears, at once humanizing the men and deepening the disillusionment with the office they held.[22]

Robespierre created an atmosphere of terror in his politicizing of private moral corruption away from Revolutionary ideals. Our own politics is, while not nearly as violent, dysfunctional. Part of the public's decline in the trust of public actors was justified, especially after the scandals of the 1960s and 1970s. But today, much of it is manufactured. In our apolitical state, the public tends to aim its judgment and assess its solutions not at impersonal laws, institutions, and issues but at the unknowable inner intentions and characters of public actors.

CAN THEATRICS CALL ATTENTION TO ISSUES?

Much as Thoreau monumentalized John Brown by equating him with Christ in order to shock his audience, political office-holders, office-seekers, social and political movements, and even non-political celebrities today must shock audiences in order to draw attention. According to the radical version of theatrical politics we covered earlier, these acts are sup-posed to bring attention away from the speaker and toward an issue that exists, as Arendt would say "outside of and between men." Thoreau, according to Jack Turner, was trying to get his audience to pay attention to the gross moral injustice of slavery, not himself, nor to John Brown as an individual. This necessitates a reliance on shocking or disrupting the audience.

There have been several examples of this type of theatrical attempt at disruption or demonstration in recent years. Yet given the prevalence of the ideal of authenticity in American political culture, the public response is more often than not immediately aimed at the characters and personalities of the protesters rather than the issues they raise. On Thursday, January 15, 2015, on Route 93 North heading into Boston, protesters from Black Lives Matter blocked rush-hour morning traffic into the city by chaining themselves to barrels they had placed in the middle of the road. They were protesting in response to the acquittal of a police officer who shot a black teenager, Michael Brown, in Ferguson, Missouri, in August of 2014. It took almost five hours for police to unchain them and remove them from the highway. One of the protesters said:

> The reason why we're holding disruptions is to effect a larger scale of economic disruption. These entire systems of policing and judicial systems are untenable, and we're here to advocate strongly. I personally feel disruptions are powerful. I feel they can wake people up a little bit from their privilege and their insulation. I personally cannot understand why killing a black child is not enough for people to stop. So that's why we're here and that's why we're doing this.[23]

Another protester stated that the protest was "necessary to disrupt a capitalist structure that has been built on the physical and economic exploitation of black bodies since our country's inception." As was discussed in our chapter on theatrical politics, this "oppositional performative contestation" was meant ultimately to bring attention to an issue through shock value and disruption, not to the persons performing the act.

The response from commuters and state officials was not as idealistic and certainly not based upon the political issue the protesters wished to have addressed. Police and commuters complained about blocking the flow of traffic (on a highway that is already infamous for traffic problems). Officials complained that it endangered lives because ambulances could not get through.[24] This is what the story was about. After the dust settled on issues of safety and inconvenience, conservative media turned not to the issue of policing (even to offer a rebuttal to the group on the specific grievance they had over Michael Brown) but to the caricatures of the group members as lazy, hypocritical hippies who inconvenienced hardworking Bostonians. Gateway Pundit, a conservative blog, ran a story about reporters going to the homes of the protesters only to find "adult children playing revolutionary while living with their rich parents." They described the attire of one of the protesters, Noah McKenna: "his hair braided in long dreadlocks ... wearing gym shorts, sandals, and a zippered sweatshirt ... looked and smelled like a dirty hippie."[25] Not surprisingly, the immediate reaction is to focus on the messenger of a political message, their motives, even their form of dress, rather than the issue itself which, in a more politicized culture, would exist "between and outside" of the individuals involved.

During the Obama presidency, we also saw theatrical displays from two quite different ideological camps: the Tea Party and Occupy Wall Street. Both of these attempted theatrics to bring attention to issues, but soon ended up casting public judgment on the characters and intentions of the actors. Lodged in the minds of Tea Party activists and the media was the fact that the name itself was based on perhaps the most folkloric performance in American history: the Boston Tea Party. There, over 300 colonists from the Sons of Liberty masqueraded as Native Americans in protest upon a ship from the British East India Company. One of the first national Tea Party events to gain widespread national attention was on "Tax Day," April 15, 2009. Conservatives in several cities around the country, including Washington D.C., donned colonial garb and decorated themselves with tea bags in order to protest spending policy—both proposed and enacted—by the Obama administration.[26] Immediately, the Tea Party's theatrics instigated praise from conservatives and disdain from liberals. From both camps was an overemphasis not on the policy issues being raised but the personal characteristics of the membership. House Speaker Nancy Pelosi branded the movement as "astroturf" because of the wealthy corporate donors she argued were bankrolling its operations.[27] Liberal bloggers and commentators painted the membership as ignorant hillbillies who could not spell (a website called "Americans Against The Tea Party" had a blog post that simply listed 20 misspelled protest signs).[28] Those on the right praised the movement by the same measurement: the personal characteristics of its membership. Rather than saying the movement was populated by ignoramuses, many conservatives praised its authenticity. Speaking at the 2010 Tea Party Convention in Nashville, Tennessee, Sarah Palin said of the Tea Party: "It is just so inspiring to see real people—not inside the Beltway professionals—come out and stand up and speak out for common-sense conservative principles."[29] It seemed that for both its supporters and its detractors, the Tea Party came to be swallowed into the same obsessions over character that animates most other would-be policy debates in American life.

The Occupy Wall Street Movement faced the same problem. It began in September 2011 and based itself primarily in Zuccotti Park in New York City. While the movement began largely as a protest against the perceived excesses of Wall Street and the connected issue of economic inequality in the United States, it was immediately criticized by those on both the left and the right for lacking a clear agenda. Even more damning was the focus on the optics of the movement. *The Washington Times* mocked the protesters as "screwball hippies."[30] Glenn Beck's *TheBlaze* spoke of protesters in tie-dyed T-shirts and star-spangled underwear.[31] A *New York Post* article interviewed people near the rallies who asked, "How can anyone take them seriously? They look like homeless people" and charged "these people need a change of wardrobe and a shower." The *Post* then focused the story on "the good laugh" the protesters provided to the "hardworking people gazing from their office window."[32] The narrative quickly became about how lazy and unkempt the protesters were, while the very real issue of economic inequality fell by the wayside.

Both the Tea Party and Occupy Wall Street eventually became branded as harmful to their own ideological interests. This was based largely on the characteristics of the members of the movements: the Tea Party for its bombast, its inability to compromise, and for its perceived racism and ignorance and Occupy Wall Street for its aimlessness, its disruptions, and the perception of it as a protest orchestrated by whiny, lazy, privileged kids with too much time on their hands. Yet what commentators miss about theatrical politics is the fact that they are successful insofar as their impact last far beyond the involvement of the members themselves. An Arendtian notion of heroic political action is impersonal; it is not concerned with whether a given political act is fashionable years after its inception, nor with whether the members are personally lauded for their activism. While the two movements have largely subsided, the policy impacts of their protests ought to be the focus of analysis. For the Tea Party, the impact is obvious: President Obama spent the vast majority of his presidency having had an opposition in Congress that was elected as a result of Tea Party passion in the midterm elections of 2010, at the height of the movement.[33] For Occupy Wall Street, the results are mixed. Yet it is undeniable that the issue of economic inequality became much more of a salient political issue in recent years. We saw this immediately in Obama's rhetoric in his 2012 reelection campaign, we saw it in Obama's ability to raise taxes on top earners shortly after the campaign, and we saw it in both the insurgent 2016 presidential campaign of Bernie Sanders and even in the rhetoric of some in the Republican Party who may never have discussed the issue just a few short years ago.[34] Thus, contemporary political analysis ought not simply to focus *exclusively* on the character of individual actors or movement members, but the long-term goals they impact.

AUTHENTICITY TODAY

American political culture's overemphasis on authenticity of political actors is problematic; it brings our judgment away from issues we face and institutions we share and toward the dark, mysterious recesses of individual selves, which we are ill-equipped to judge. Authenticity remains as an ideal, but without a framework for how to define it or achieve it. In the 1950s, national, widely read publications would feature covers and headlines investigating the nature of selfhood in an affluent society. The 1960s counterculture movements and the self-help crazes of the following decades gave many answers to those investigations, often either through providing spiritual resources for self-realization or through consumer products that were designed to make individuals feel unique. Several decades after the issue took on cultural and political importance in both popular culture and academia, why ought authenticity be an issue of concern once again? Has not the concept of authenticity become so subjective, so undefinable, and used for such shallow or even nefarious purposes that it ought not to concern us as a political goal, or even a goal against which to measure other modes of politics? Further, especially with the onslaught of social media, with its constantly growing options for identity presentation and its dominance by marketing interests, can modern men and women claim a unique, authentic self apart from their peers and the structures and institutions? In other words, why is authenticity still important, and why now?

It is precisely at this moment that authenticity becomes an even more pressing area of attention and study. Facebook and especially Twitter, for instance, have served as venues for organized political action, from the Arab Springs to the Tea Party to Occupy Wall Street to Trumpism. Since social capital theorists like Robert Putnam wrote about the ill effects of "technological transformation of leisure" two decades ago (namely, the passivity that pervaded American society after the invention of television), new technologies have resulted not in general passivity, but have generated *interactivity* instead.[35] While this is an improvement for partisans of a more interactive public, how much does it fulfill the participatory, democratic Enlightenment ideals of Rousseau or the counter-culture ideas of the Esalen Institute? In other words, does contemporary social media contribute to the formation of more autonomous selves, and do those autonomous selves then somehow remake the social or political world? While these questions are beyond the scope of this book, further work in political theory should continue to consider the role of technology and social media on the authentic self and the performative self.

In this book, we have explored the argument that the best type of politics needs to find a middle ground between authenticity, theatricality, and institutional politics, which I find most evident in the politics and the self-practices of Henry David Thoreau and Abraham Lincoln. Moral, effective political action does not always mean saying exactly what one believes, nor does it always mean shielding one's true intentions. It does not mean being unconditionally compassionate to all of humanity, yet it also does not mean dealing with one's neighbors merely through the prism of shared political processes and institutions, where legal citizenship is the only commonality. And it does not mean that we ought to be bound up as one tight-knit community in our political identities, but also that we are not completely opaque to one another and that bonds and coalitions can be formed from time to time around common moral goals. Thoreau's political life in time shows us ways to incorporate the best of authenticity and theatricality. His philosophy on written communication transcends the gap between poetic-romantic authorship and disengaged, distant authorship. Thoreau offers us a way, through communicative writing, to connect with our natural selves at the individual level, while sharing common bonds of humanity. And Lincoln shows us how we can gradually alter existing laws and institutions toward moral goals without engaging in counterproductive radicalism that seeks to tear down the rule of law.

It is the view of this author that our political culture is disserved by those who hold political actors to absolute standards of morality and authenticity, which are impossible to judge. I take this view not only because it is such a lackadaisical way to engage in political engagement, but that it assumes too much about our ability to psychoanalyze public figures. All humans are, at points in time, hypocrites who hold different standards for different individuals, allowing some individuals to escape their moral judgment as long as they agree with their ideologies. To say otherwise is to impose a totalitarian iron band around the fluctuations of our inner selves, and our public, democratic politics.

We can see in numerous examples that our political culture is still infused with the standard of authenticity-as-legitimacy, at least in the reporting and discussion of statements by public actors. We have seen throughout this book both the conceptual and practical difficulties inherent in our overemphasis on scrutinizing the actor behind the act. Public judgment of private selves keeps the polis at a standstill; politics becomes nothing more than a debate over internal characters rather than as a space for citizen education, debate, and ultimately compromise on issues upon which we can disagree. We are seeing this play out in the tribal warfare that politics has become under Trumpism. At best, our focus on intentionality is a symptom of a depoliticized mass society. At worst, it is a warning sign of an ever-possible totalitarian ideology that seeks to replace institutions with cults of personality. Our challenge, which is a somewhat unmeasurable question, is whether the right combination of moral authenticity, moderate theatricality, and democratic institutional norms can push us toward greater understanding and more elevated debate over difficult issues in the long run.

A century from now, all of the members of the Tea Party, Occupy Wall Street, Black Lives Matter, Barack Obama, Donald Trump, and all the other movements and personalities of this era will be gone. Few will judge these characters as intensely as we do now, and even fewer will be offended by their inner intentions. But toward what kind of public life and public policies that spring from that political culture will their actions have led? While Lincoln was seen as a bumbling backwoodsman, he is lauded as a national hero today for keeping the country together. And while Thoreau had been seen by many, especially in academics, as an apolitical gadfly who did nothing to stop slavery, he is increasingly monumentalized a century and a half later as a great example of a conscientious citizen, one who lives to improve one's soul while finding occasional spaces to wake up his neighbors to their own inner consciences. The Enlightenment project has always been dedicated to mobilizing the public in fits and starts toward greater achievement of private individuality while directing public action in concert toward the solution of shared problems. Perhaps this combination can teach us something today as we seek to identify and rectify the next great moral issues together, apart, and alone with ourselves.

Notes

1. Hannah Arendt, *The Origins of Totalitarianism* (New York: Harcourt, Brace & World, 1966), 382.
2. Garet Williams, "Trump's conspiracy-filled interview with Fox & Friends," *Vox*, June 23, 2017, https://www.vox.com/policy-and-politics/2017/6/23/15861628/trump-fox-comey-mueller-tapes-clinton-conspiracy.
3. Alexandra Jaffe, "Kellyanne Conway: WH Spokesman Gave 'Alternative Facts' on Inauguration Crowd," *NBC News*, https://www.nbcnews.com/storyline/meet-the-press-70-years/wh-spokesman-gave-alternative-facts-inauguration-crowd-n710466.
4. Lydia Saad, "Trump Sets New Low Point for Inaugural Approval Rating," *Gallup*, http://news.gallup.com/poll/202811/trump-sets-new-low-point-inaugural-approval-rating.aspx.
5. Eric Levitz, "Trump Campaign Manager on False Report of Clinton Indictment: 'The Damage Is Done'," *New York Magazine*, November 4, 2016. http://nymag.com/daily/intelligencer/2016/11/conway-on-fox-clinton-indictment-story-the-damage-is-done.html.
6. Glenn Kessler, Salvador Rizzo, and Meg Kelly, "President Trump has made 3001 false or misleading claims so far," *The Washington Post*, May 1, 2018, https://www.washingtonpost.com/news/fact-checker/wp/2018/05/01/president-trump-has-made-3001-false-or-misleading-claims-so-far/.
7. "Declining trust in government is denting democracy," *The Economist*, January 25, 2017, https://www.economist.com/blogs/graphicdetail/2017/01/daily-chart-20.
8. "Distrust of politicians helped fuel Brexit vote, report finds," *Daily Gazette Standard*, January 24, 2017, http://www.gazette-news.co.uk/news/national/15045125.Distrust_of_politicians_helped_fuel_Brexit_vote__report_finds/.
9. Yascha Mounk, *The People vs. Democracy: Why Our Freedom Is in Danger and How to Save It* (Harvard University Press, 2018), 2.
10. Andrew Sullivan, "Democracies end when they are too democratic," *New York Magazine*, May 1, 2016, http://nymag.com/daily/intelligencer/2016/04/america-tyranny-donald-trump.html.
11. Martin Gilens and Benjamin I. Page, "Testing Theories of American Politics: Elites, Interest Groups, and Average Citizens," Perspectives on Politics 12, no. 3 (September 2014): 577.
12. Diana C. Mutz, "Status threat, not economic hardship, explains the 2016 presidential vote," *Proceedings of the National Academy of Sciences*, April 2018.

13. "Is American democracy really in decline? A debate." interview of Yascha Mounk by Ezra Klein, *The Ezra Klein Show*, 4/30/2018, Audio 0:00, https://art19.com/shows/the-ezra-klein-show/episodes/eeeadb50-131d-4699-b1db-0d984518e2da.
14. Mounk, Interview, Audio 17:27.
15. Mounk, Interview, Audio 35:19.
16. Ron Suskind, "Faith, Certainty and the Presidency of George W. Bush," *The New York Times Magazine*, October 17, 2004, https://www.nytimes.com/2004/10/17/magazine/faith-certainty-and-the-presidency-of-george-w-bush.html.
17. David Limbaugh, "Is Obama Intentionally Destroying America?," *WND*, July 09, 2012, http://www.wnd.com/2012/07/is-obama-intentionally-destroying-america/.
18. "The Century of the Self (Full Documentary)," YouTube video, posted by "David Lessig" July 9, 2015, https://www.youtube.com/watch?v=eJ3Rz GoQC4s. All "The Century of the Self" quotes from this clip.
19. *The Century of the Self.*
20. *The Century of the Self.*
21. Julian Zelizer, "Distrustful Americans Still Live in Age of Watergate," *CNN*, July 07, 2014, http://www.cnn.com/2014/07/07/opinion/zelizer-watergate-politics/index.html.
22. Ken Burns and Lynn Novick, "How the Vietnam War Broke the American Presidency," *The Atlantic*, October 2017, https://www.theatlantic.com/magazine/archive/2017/10/how-americans-lost-faith-in-the-presidency/537897/.
23. "Protesters Block Traffic on I-93 North and South of Boston," *Boston Globe*, January 15, 2015, https://www.bostonglobe.com/news/local/massachusetts/2015/01/15/protesters-block-traffic-north-and-south-boston/WTAdtRy4FIoPTOgIAqQE0H/story.html.
24. Peter Schworm, Laura Crimaldi and John R. Ellement, "Protesters Snarl Morning Commute on I-93 near Boston." *Boston Globe*, January 15, 2015, https://www.bostonglobe.com/metro/2015/01/15/protesters-block-traffic-southeast-express-northbound/G3aLvpDWRixI2I6SVyaErM/story.html.
25. Kristinn Taylor, "White #BlackLivesMatter Boston Protesters Found Living with Parents in Luxury Mansions," *The Gateway Pundit*, January 18, 2015, https://www.thegatewaypundit.com/2015/01/white-black-livesmatter-boston-protesters-found-living-with-parents-in-luxury-mansions/.
26. Liz Robbins, "Tax Day Is Met With Tea Parties," *The New York Times*, April 15, 2009, https://www.nytimes.com/2009/04/16/us/politics/16taxday.html.

27. "Pelosi and the Tea Party 'Share Views'" *ABC News*, February 28, 2010, http://blogs.abcnews.com/thenote/2010/02/pelosi-and-the-tea-party-share-views.html.
28. "20 More Hysterical Misspelled Tea Party Signs! (Image Gallery)," *Americans Against the Tea Party*, July 07, 2013, http://aattp.org/20-more-hysterical-misspelled-tea-party-signs-image-gallery/.
29. Sarah Palin, "Tea Party Convention Keynote Speech (complete Transcript Audio Video)," *American Rhetoric Online Speech Bank*, February 06, 2010, http://www.americanrhetoric.com/speechessarahpalin2010teapartykeynote.htm.
30. James S. Robbins, "TRR: Screwball Hippies Think the Marines Are Coming," *The Washington Times*, October 01, 2011, https://www.washingtontimes.com/blog/robbins-report/2011/oct/1/screwball-hippies-think-marines-are-coming/.
31. Billy Hallowell, "AP Analyzes 'Days of Rage': It's Unclear Exactly What the Demonstrators Want," *TheBlaze*, October 01, 2011, https://www.theblaze.com/news/2011/10/01/ap-analyzes-days-of-rage-its-unclear-exactly-what-the-demonstrators-want.
32. Frank Rosario, "OWS Bums Are a Big Joke," *New York Post*, May 02, 2012, https://nypost.com/2012/05/02/ows-bums-are-a-big-joke/.
33. Jeffrey Jones, "Americans See Positive, Negative Effects of Tea Party Movement," *Gallup*, November 04, 2010, http://news.gallup.com/poll/144242/americans-positive-negative-effects-tea-party-movement.aspx.
34. Brendan Nyhan, "Why Republicans Are Suddenly Talking About Economic Inequality," *The New York Times*, February 13, 2015, https://www.nytimes.com/2015/02/14/upshot/why-republicans-are-suddenly-talking-about-economic-inequality.html.
35. See Robert D. Putnam, *Bowling Alone: The Collapse and Revival of American Community* (New York: Simon & Schuster, 2000).

Printed by Printforce, the Netherlands